WHAT PEOPLE AF

IRISH PA

'There are very few books out there written on Celtic Reconstructionism and Morgan Daimler's book on Irish Reconstructionism is a welcome addition. The book is a well-researched look at the basics and should serve as a great introductory text for people interested in walking this path who don't know where to start.'

Maya St. Clair, editor and contributor to Air n-Aithesc, a peer-reviewed CR journal

'Morgan Daimler has written the kind of book I wish I'd been able to write 20 years ago. She addresses many of the things I've been writing about for years, and does so succinctly and cogently. Her approach is clear and practical, and she provides good sources for her work. This is sure to be an essential reference for anyone interested in reconstructing the polytheist practices of ancient Ireland, and of other Celtic cultures.'

Erynn Rowan Laurie, author of *Ogam: Weaving Word Wisdom* and *A Circle of Stones*

'Morgan Daimler has given us an excellent, honest approach to reconstructing Irish Paganism, dispelling common misconceptions and explaining the path in simple, easy-to-read terms. The book is both a superb introduction and a excellent reference to the beliefs, practices and studies of the CR way. The author explains the subject clearly and makes it obvious where the views expressed are hers alone and leaves us to choose what to follow, study and practice. With pronunciation guides in Old and Modern Irish, a recommended reading list and bibliography for further study for the uninitiated, *Pagan Portals: Irish Paganism*

is a must-have book for your book shelf – virtual or otherwise!'
Gary & Ruth Colcombe, from the Celtic Myth Podshow"

'Irish Reconstructionist Polytheism introduces the reader to a path which is growing in popularity, in a clear, concise and grounded way. The book explains the importance of academic research and balances it with personal experience as well as conjuring the mystical nature of IRP, making the book accessible and relevant to those who are curious and those who practice. For myself, I wish I could have had this book as a resource many years ago.'
Jane Brideson, artist and blogger at The Ever-Living Ones – Irish Goddesses & Gods in landscape, myth & custom

'Morgan Daimler's lucid introduction to polytheist reconstruction as related to Gaelic polytheist traditions is valuable to both beginners and those who have been worshiping the gods for years.'
C. Lee Vermeers, author of *Teagasca: The Instructions of Cormac Mac Airt*, and co-author of the CR FAQs

'It is an excellent introduction to the topic, one of the first written, which touches on the main beliefs and themes found among Irish Reconstructionists, in a way that will enable the reader to begin well equipped on an Irish Reconstructionist path.'
Segomâros Widugeni, formerly **Aedh Rua** author of *Celtic Flame*

Pagan Portals
Irish Paganism

Reconstructing Irish Polytheism

Pagan Portals
Irish Paganism

Reconstructing Irish Polytheism

Morgan Daimler

Winchester, UK
Washington, USA

First published by Moon Books, 2015
Moon Books is an imprint of John Hunt Publishing Ltd., Laurel House, Station Approach,
Alresford, Hants, SO24 9JH, UK
office1@jhpbooks.net
www.johnhuntpublishing.com
www.moon-books.net

For distributor details and how to order please visit the 'Ordering' section on our website.

Text copyright: Morgan Daimler 2014

ISBN: 978 1 78535 145 7
Library of Congress Control Number: 2015937454

A CIP catalogue record for this book is available from the British Library.

Design: Stuart Davies

Printed and bound by CPI Group (UK) Ltd, Croydon, CR0 4YY, UK

We operate a distinctive and ethical publishing philosophy in all
areas of our business, from our global network of authors to
production and worldwide distribution.

CONTENTS

Author's Note

I have been pagan since 1991 and following what I would call an Irish Reconstructionist path since about 1994. However, it wasn't until the late 1990s that I found other people with similar interests in combining academia and religion. It was not until into the 2000s that I first heard of the term 'Celtic Reconstructionist Polytheism' and realized that described what I was doing. Part of the reason for this is that there simply weren't, and still aren't, many resources for this path. People drawn to using a Reconstructionist approach to Irish paganism are left, for the most part, to figure things out on their own and piece together practices as they go. Although there are more online resources today than there were 20 years ago, and a couple of books out now, it remains a religious approach that is mostly left to the individual to figure out. I am hopeful that this is changing and that more and more books will be released that look at Irish Reconstructionism, what it is, and how to do it.

All deity names and general terms in this book are presented in modern Irish; however, Appendix A includes the Old Irish names as well as pronunciations in both languages. There are also quotes given from the source material in the original languages. As with all of my books, citations will be done in APA format.

In writing this book as a brief introduction I am hoping to serve two main purposes: to offer a resource to people who are interested in Irish Reconstructionist Polytheism as a practice and to give those curious about what it is, a good basic understanding of it. I also believe it will serve as a useful resource for anyone interested in Irish Polytheism, even if they are not Reconstructionists.

Morgan Daimler
March 20, 2015

Chapter 1

Basics of Irish Reconstructionist Polytheism

Bennacht dé ocus ainde fort
Táin Bó Cúailgne
(Blessing of the Gods and not-Gods on you)

What is Reconstructionism?

Reconstruction is a methodology that uses a variety of sources including archaeology, anthropology, mythology, folklore, and historical texts to reconstruct what an ancient belief or practice most likely would have been like. Using this reconstruction of the old, the belief or practice can then be adapted for modern use. Or, as I like to say, reconstruction is understanding the old pagan religion so that we can envision what it would have been like if it had never been interrupted by foreign influences and had continued to exist until today.

Reconstructionism is most often applied to spirituality, but it can be used for a variety of related practices including traditional non-religious witchcraft. It can also be used for mystic practices used in conjunction with spiritual practices, such as the reconstruction of seership methods within Irish Reconstructionism, or of seidhr within Heathenry. Reconstruction is a method that is applied to a wide array of different ancient pagan faiths including Norse, Anglo-Saxon, Minoan, Egyptian, Irish, Gaulish, and Indo-European[1] to name just a few. It is a method that is both sound and flexible, but which also requires personal engagement and imagination. Because of this, the end results of different people's reconstruction of the same culture's religion will not be identical, although they should be similar.

In this particular case, the methodology of reconstruction is being applied to Irish Polytheism, hence the name of this approach to Irish paganism. What this means in practical terms is that it is a spiritual structure based on studying archaeology, anthropology, mythology and so on, specifically of Ireland, focusing on the pagan period and any traces of pagan beliefs during the Christian period. Obviously there are certain challenges with this, including the fact that we have nothing written by the pagan Irish themselves, so we must not only reconstruct the old beliefs, but also seek to filter out any foreign influences. Academic material has two main approaches to the subject of pagan Irish beliefs, which are diametrically opposed and tend to be held strongly. The first is the nativist view, which says that Irish mythology and culture were influenced by pre-Christian pagan paradigms and reflect genuine ancient beliefs that were preserved as such by later scholars. The second view is the anti-nativist, which says that the preserved material we have in the mythology was preserved through Christian mediators who themselves were influenced by both Christian and Classical views and therefore it must be assumed that all preserved material reflects some degree of foreign influence and does not show us genuine pre-Christian beliefs. As an Irish Reconstructionist studying the source material you will encounter both approaches.

Aspects of Irish Reconstructionism:

1. Study: Any form of reconstruction requires some level of study. It's important to familiarize yourself with the ancient pagan culture in order to understand it well enough to create viable modern practices from it. There is a wide variety of books available on Iron Age Irish culture, pagan Irish culture, Irish folk beliefs, and archaeology in Ireland that can all be used as source material.

2. Discernment: Speaking of source material, another important aspect of reconstruction is critical thinking. It's

important to be able to tell a good source from a bad one and judge the value of any material you are reading or hearing about. Commonsense is one aspect of discernment, but another is healthy skepticism; nothing should be accepted automatically as true just because it is in a book. Rather a reader should assess the value of the material based on how sound it is – how provably true the material is – how persuasive the evidence is, and whether the author backs up their idea with solid evidence.

3. Language: There's a saying in Irish: 'Tir gan teanga, tir gan anam' (A nation without a language, a nation without a soul).[2] I think this reflects a core truth, that our language is not only a basic means of communication, but also an expression of how we relate to and perceive reality. In psychology we call this linguistic relativity,[3] the idea that language affects how we think about the world. What this means in practical terms is that to truly understand a culture you must understand the language of that culture. As an Irish polytheist it is important to at least try to understand the language, for a variety of reasons. There is much insight and truth to be gained from reading the old myths, but there is a catch, because the translations that are available are written through a very specific lens that distorts and changes what it reflects in ways that we are often not aware of. Reading the original language[4] gives us a more direct understanding of the story as it would have been understood originally. The Irish language is also part of the living Irish culture, and its preservation is a cultural issue, which we as polytheists following Irish Gods should care about. Finally, there is something visceral and primal about connecting to our Gods in the language of their own native culture.

4. Practice: Research is the tool to build the structure of the religion being reconstructed, but the purpose of doing that is to then move forward into actual practice. This includes an array of things from celebrating holy days to offering rites. The ultimate point is to create something that is a completely viable in the modern world, but is based on the ancient beliefs and practices. Each Reconstructionist will create a slightly different vision of what this modern practice looks like and is, but they should all have similarities.

5. The living culture: One final aspect of Irish Reconstructionism is interaction with the modern living culture, which in this case would be Irish culture. This can include appreciation of Irish music, art, literature, food, and current events.

Common Myths About Reconstructionism

I've said it before, but it bears repeating: Reconstructionism is a very misunderstood thing. There are many reasons for why that is and why some of those misunderstandings keep being perpetuated, but mostly it comes down to assumptions and stereotypes. So to start let's take a look at some common misconceptions and realities of Reconstructionism in general.

1. Reconstructionists are not mean

Well, they aren't any meaner, generally speaking, than any other community can seem to outsiders. I see this one all the time, and it is usually rooted in two things: a difference in communication style and a difference in paradigm. People within Reconstructionist communities tend to have a communication style – in my experience – that is rather blunt and straightforward. In contrast, people within non-Reconstructionist communities tend, again in my experience, to have communication styles that favor friendly language and more passive-aggressive approaches. Reconstructionists tend to operate from a paradigm of earned respect, skepticism, and an expectation of support for statements, while non-Reconstructionists have a paradigm of immediate intimacy, trust, and acceptance of people's assertions on face value. Neither of these is inherently better or worse than the other, but they create very different cultures and expectations of behavior for the people within them. It should be obvious that these communication styles and paradigms are in many ways antithetical and it is almost inevitable that people interacting between the two groups will have issues with each other.

2. Reconstructionists are not re-enactors

This is another very common one, usually expressed through the criticism that Reconstructionism is flawed because 'there are things that should be left in the past'. Well, yes, clearly. No one is advocating the return of human sacrifice or slavery – although we are honest about the fact that these were historic practices and that understanding them is important to understanding the culture. Reconstruction is not about recreating ancient religion exactly as it was and practicing it that way, but about understanding how it was in order to make it viable today.

I, for one, love indoor plumbing and refrigeration, and I'm not about to give up all modern amenities to build a roundhouse and pretend I'm living in the Iron Age. I might not mind a round-house with wifi and solar panels though. Obviously, just like the rest of the population, there are some Reconstructionists who do favor sustainable living, off-the-grid living, and even a rejection of many aspects of modern technology, but that isn't an aspect of reconstruction itself, any more than belonging to the Society for Creative Anachronism (SCA) or going to Renn Faires is.

3. *Reconstructionists are not armchair pagans*

It is true that there is a bit of a hesitance in Reconstructionist groups – or at least the ones I have experience with – to discuss actual practice and experience. I think there are several reasons for this, including the fact that we tend to get very tangential about minutia in discussions and we get sidetracked when someone else starts disagreeing and saying their research supports a different approach. However, just because we don't talk all the time about what we actually do in our daily lives doesn't mean we aren't doing anything. In the same way a non-Reconstructionist may talk a lot about what they do and not much about what they read, but that doesn't mean that they don't read anything (I like to assume anyway). Reconstructionists do like their source material, but the entire point of the source material is using it to create a viable practice.

4. *Reconstructionists don't hate unverified personal gnosis (UPG)*[5]

This one is also often expressed as 'Reconstructionists are obsessed with lore' or 'Reconstructionists are pagan fundamentalists'. However you say it, it simply isn't true. And that's not just my opinion, I'll quote the CR FAQs here, under What is Celtic Reconstruction (CR):

> By studying the old manuscript sources and the regional folklore, combining this information *with mystical and ecstatic practice*, and working together to weed out the non-Celtic elements that can arise, we are nurturing what still lives and helping the polytheistic Celtic traditions grow strong and whole again. (Emphasis mine.)

Incorporating personal experience and mystical practice is part of Reconstructionism, so Reconstructionists obviously do not hate personal gnosis. However, we do apply the same critical thinking and discernment to mystical experiences as we do to any source of information and I suspect this is where the problem comes in. Reconstructionists question everything to ascertain its veracity including spiritual experiences and that is often unpopular especially in communities that do not share the same approach.

But seriously people, Reconstructionists don't hate mystical experiences, nor do we reject anything that isn't straight out of a book. We just place a lot of value on the vast amount of combined experience and belief that is the culture we are reconstructing and we use that as a measure for the credibility of new information.

Reconstruction is not a methodology for everyone, just like any other path it is simply one option among many. It appeals to certain people for a variety of reasons, and leaves other people uninterested, and that's okay. Many people who don't practice Reconstructionism, and even some who do, misunderstand what it is and sometimes perpetuate stereotypes about it. I hope this helped at least a little bit to shed some light on a few of them. Reconstructionists aren't out to make people cry, aren't trying to recreate the Iron Age, aren't only about reading books, and aren't against personal ecstatic experiences or gnosis. What we are about is using solid academic evidence and personal inspiration to envision what that Polytheism would have looked like today if it had existed without interruption. We are about honoring our ancestors, spirits of diverse types, and Gods. We are about respecting and helping to preserve the living culture today.

Reconstruction isn't about living looking backwards. It's about walking forward with the past a firm path beneath our feet, guiding our steps.

Chapter 2

What Are the Beliefs?

Bíaidh doberad ar ndee ocus ar dtoicthe dúinn.
Fragmentary Annals
(We'll have what our Gods and fate bring us.)

There are no hard and fast beliefs within Irish Reconstructionist Polytheism, but there are some that are commonly held, and that is what we will look at here. As with most aspects of Reconstructionism though, different people can look at the same evidence and draw different conclusions so sometimes these beliefs will vary from group to group or person to person. It can be said though that Irish Reconstructionist Polytheists do have these basic beliefs: Polytheism, animism, belief in honoring spirits and ancestors, immortality of the soul, and shared cosmology.

Irish Reconstructionist Polytheism is a polytheist and animist belief system. What this means in practical terms is that people who use this methodology to shape a pagan religion from older Irish pagan beliefs believe in many Gods who are all unique individuals and also that all things have a spirit. This plays out in practice in the acknowledgement and honoring of different Irish Gods, often members of the Tuatha Dé Danann, and of Otherworldly spirits, spirits of the land, and ancestral spirits.

The Tuatha Dé Danann are generally considered to be the Gods of Ireland. While we do not have any primary sources for the pagan Irish we have an abundance of secondary sources. We have mythology preserved by early scribes during and immediately after the conversion period and we have later folklore that preserved the memory of deities in certain areas. Archaeology is a significant tool as well, as studying archaeological sites can tell

10

us where ritual centers were and whether areas from myth and folklore did have ritual significance. We know from these sites that the Gods honored there were worshiped with offerings, and stories such as *De Gabáil in t-Sída* imply that such offerings were necessary for the people to receive blessing and abundance. We can also study place names and the way that folklore around specific deities focuses at a location. The different Tuatha Dé Danann had their own sacred places and real world sites that belonged to them. Like putting together pieces of a jigsaw puzzle, no single piece gives us an answer, but when we put them all together we see the bigger picture.

The following is an annotated list of some of the more popular or well-known Irish Gods and highlights of their mythology and beliefs associated with them. This list is by no means complete and is meant only to offer a sample of some of the deities worshiped; people interested in Irish Polytheism are strongly encouraged to read the mythology as well as books such as O hOgain's *The Lore of Ireland* to gain a better idea of the full range of the pantheon.

Áine

They came out of the fairy mound with Éogabul son of Durgabul king of the fairy mound after them and Aine daughter of Éogabul with a bronze timpán in her hand playing before him... That girl's name is on the hill, that is, Áine Chlíach.
Cath Maige Mucrama

Called Áine Chliar, often translated as Áine of the wisps, but possibly means Áine of Clui.[6] Her name means 'bright' or 'shining' and many people relate her to the sun, crops, and love because of the different stories in which she has a mortal lover. Áine had a hill in Limerick called Cnoc Áine, which is her home. She was said to be the divine ancestor of the Eoghanacht family and the FitzGeralds, and likely a land and sovereignty Goddess who granted legitimacy to rulers in that area (O hOgain, 2006). She has strong ties to the holiday of Lúnasa, when it is said she becomes the consort of Crom Cruach[7] for three days, during which time she may be associated with the excessive heat of late July and early August (MacNeill, 1962).

While her role at Lúnasa is antagonistic towards people, she is generally seen as positive, and there is a longstanding tradition at Midsummer of honoring her on her hill with a torch-lit procession. Clumps of straw would be lit and carried to the top of the hill before being scattered in the cultivated fields, with the belief that they would bring blessing and abundance (O hOgain, 2006). Modern practitioners who honor Áine often relate to her as a Goddess of the summer sun or representing the sun's power and may look to her for abundance. Her sister Grian, a more obscure Goddess whose name means 'sun', has a sí near Áine's and some scholars see her balancing her sister and representing the winter sun (Ellis, 1987).

Badhbh

H-i Ross Bodbo .i. na Morrighno, ar iss ed a ross-side Crich Roiss ocus iss i an bodb catha h-i ocus is fria id-beurur bee Neid .i. bandee in catæ, uair is inann be Neid ocus dia cath.
Tochmarch Emire
(In the Wood of Badb, that is of the Morrigu, therefore her proven-wood the land of Ross, and she is the Battle-Crow and is also called the woman of Neit, that is Goddess of Battle, because Neit is also a God of Battle.)

She does not have an epithet per se, but is known as 'Badhbh Chatha' (battle crow), as one of the meanings for her name is 'crow'. Badhbh (Old Irish Badb) appears in a variety of Irish myths usually associated with battle, death, and prophecy. In the

Cath Maige Tuired Cunga a bard among the Fir Bolg says that the red-mouthed Badhbh will rejoice at the slaughter, and she is often referred to in this way and described as enjoying the carnage of the battlefield. Although she can be quite fearsome she is also beneficial in battle as those she favors tend to win (O hOgain, 2006). Badhbh is one of the sisters of the Morrigan in the *Lebor Gabála Érenn* and is called one of the three Morrignae in Sanas Cormac. Her name, like that of the Morrigan, is also a title that is sometimes applied to other deities. Badhbh is also associated with the image of the washer woman, as she appears in some stories washing the bloody clothes and armor of those doomed to die. Some modern worshipers avoid Badhbh, but others embrace her as a Goddess to be honored in difficult times and in relation to prophecy work. Offerings to her in a modern context might include whiskey, blood,[8] or feeding wild crows or ravens.

Brighid

Brigit .i. banfile...bandea no adratis filid.
Sanas Cormac
(Brighid, that is a poetess...a Goddess poets used to worship)

Brighid (Old Irish Brig) is a complex Goddess who is sometimes seen as three sisters all named Brighid, based on an entry in Sanas Cormac. She or they are described as relating to poetry, healing, and smithcraft (Sanas Cormac, n.d.). The *Lebor Gabála Érenn* tells us that she had two oxen and a pig who would cry out when there was pillaging or rape in the land (Macalister, 1940). In the *Cath Maige Tuired* we learn that Brighid was the first person to ever caoine[9] in Ireland, after the death of her son Ruadan. She is an extremely popular Goddess. She is associated with both fire and water, as her modern Christian equivalent, Saint Brigid, has a perpetual flame and holy well in Kildare. Brighid is strongly associated with the holiday of Imbolc,

13

although it is worth noting that the mythology of the Goddess and that of the saint are often blurred together. Modern practitioners may honor Brighid as a deity of healing, poetry, creativity, grief (for being the first to mourn), and protection. There is a prayer called the Genealogy of Brighid that calls on her for protection and blessing. Offerings to her may include dairy products, poetry, and hand-made items.

Daghdha

There was a wondrous king over the Tuatha Dé in Ireland, Dagán by name [i.e. 'the Dagda']. Great was his power, even over the sons of Mil after they had seized the land. For the Tuatha Dé blighted the grain and the milk of the sons of Mil until they made a treaty [cairdes] with the Dagda. Thereafter they preserved their grain and their milk for them.

Celtic Heroic Age

The Daghdha (Old Irish Dagda) is one of the most well known Gods of the Tuatha Dé Danann. His epithets include 'Eochaid Ollathair' (horseman great-father), 'Aedh Álainn' (fiery shining one), and 'Ruadh Rófheasa' (red-man of great knowledge) (O hOgain, 2006). The Daghdha was seen as a very wise deity and one with authority; in one version of the *De Gabáil in t-Sída* it is the Daghdha who divides the sí among the Gods after the Gaels win Ireland and it is he who the Gaels must appeal to in order to find out what to do to flourish in the new land. He possessed several magical items including a cauldron that was one of the four treasures the Gods brought with them from the Otherworld, a harp whose playing could change the seasons, and a club that could kill with one end and give life with the other. The Daghdha is described in gigantic terms, being physically large, generous, and having a huge appetite for both food and sex. He was one of the kings of the Tuatha Dé Danann and appears to have been a popular

God historically, whose descriptions of swiftness may relate to the speed with which he was believed to respond to prayers (O hOgain, 2006). Many modern Irish Polytheists honor the Daghdha for his wisdom, skill, and ability to provide abundance.

Dian Cécht

'Os tusai, a Dien-cecht,' or Lug, 'cia cumogg conicid si em?'

'Ni anse', ol sie: 'Nach fer gentor ann, acht mona bentor a cedn de, nó min tesctar srebonn a inchinde no a smir sentuinde bodh ogslaun limsu 'sin cath arabharoch'.

Cath Maige Tuired

('And you, oh Dian Cécht,' said Lugh. 'What power as far as your half?'

'Not difficult,' he said. 'Each man wounded here, except his head is cut off from his neck, or a membrane of his brain is hacked, or the marrow of his spinal cord sharply severed, will return to battle the next day.')

Dian Cécht is the pre-eminent physician of the Gods and is described in multiple texts from the 8th through 10th centuries as a God of swift healing (O hOgain, 2006). He is portrayed in mythology healing both alone, with his sons and daughter, and in concert with Credne, the wright when he fashioned a new arm of silver for Nuadha. He is probably most well known today for helping to heal Nuadha,[10] but he also plays a significant role in the battle of Maige Tuired where he and his children heal the injured warriors so they can return to battle. Dian Cécht possessed a great healing well, the Sláine, into which he had placed every healing herb known in the world; he is also associated with destroying serpents, such as those who infested the heart of Meiche, which may have represented plague (O hOgain, 2006). Modern Irish Polytheists may honor him as a healer and find healing herbs a good offering for him.

Fliodhais

Flidais... Though slender she destroyed young men. She decreed hard close fighting.
Banshenchus

Her epithet is 'foltchaoin' (soft haired). She appears in several stories as the owner of magical cattle and deer who give milk as cows would, and both deer and cows are referred to as her kine.11 In the *Táin Bó Flidais* it is said she had a magical cow who could feed 300 men from one milking and in the *Táin Bó Cúailnge* she fed the entire army of Connacht once a week with milk from her herd (*Leabar na h-Uidre*, nd). In this story as well we learn of Fliodhais's sexual prowess as she alone could satisfy her lover Fergus; without her it would take seven women to do the same (O hOgain, 2006). The *Lebor Gabála Érenn* tells us that she was the mother of many children, some associated with farming and some with witchcraft. There is at least one reference to Flidais as a healer; in the *Táin Bó Flidais* it is said that she tended to and healed the men wounded in battle (*Leabhar na h-Uidre*, nd). Interestingly, this may relate to a more modern folk charm against poison that calls on 'Fleithas', a name similar to the modern Irish Fliodhais. This charm refers to the hounds of Fliethas, as well as the three daughters of Fleithas (Wilde, 1991). Modern Irish Polytheists may choose to honor Fliodhais as a deity of abundance; milk seems to be an appropriate offering for her.

Goibniu

Goibniu who was not impotent in smelting.
Lebor Gabala Erenn

His name is derived from the word for smith; Old Irish 'gobha', Modern Irish 'gabha' (O hOgain, 2006). It is said that he could forge a weapon with only three blows from his hammer (Ellis, 1987). Goibniu had a special drink, a mead or ale called the fled Goibnenn, which conveyed the gift of youth and immortality to the Tuatha Dé Danann (O hOgain, 2006). This drink is sometimes called the feast of Goibniu and is said in some sources to cure disease (Monaghan, 2004). He also owned a cow who gave endless milk (O hOgain, 2006). He also has some association with healing according to the St. Gall Incantation in which he is invoked to remove a thorn, possible also a reference to healing a battle wound. He is also appealed to for protection in some early Irish charms, which call on the art of Goibniu (O hOgain, 2006). This may relate to the idea that the being that created the weapon which caused the injury had power over the injury caused, something that we see in the charms relating to elf-shot.

In modern practice Goibniu is still seen as a smith God, but he also has overtones associated with the Otherworld and the sidhe, as do most of the Tuatha De. He could be called on to heal injuries caused by bladed weapons and possibly also by other weapons, and might be called on in conjunction with his two brothers by those who create with metal. I have called on him to bless weapons. Offerings to him might include beer, ale, or mead; I often offer him water, personally, as to me it makes sense to offer something cooling and refreshing to a God of the hot forge.

Lugh

Conid and rocan Lug an cétal-so síos, for lethcois ocus letsúil timchel fer n-Erenn.
(So that upon his cloak Lugh sang this to intervene, on one foot and one eye, encompassing the men of Ireland.)

His epithets include 'Ildanach' (many talented), 'Samhildanach' (having all skills), and 'Lamhfada' (long arm). Lugh (Old Irish

Lug) was a child of a Fomorian mother and Tuatha Dé Danann father who was prophesied to kill his Fomorian grandfather, the formidable Balor of the Evil Eye. Lugh accomplished this during the second battle of Maige Tuired when he put out Balor's eye with a sling stone. Lugh is the leader of the Tuatha Dé Danann during the battle against the Fomorians and is king after Naudha (Grey, 1983; Macalister, 1940).

He possessed one of the four treasures the Gods brought into the world with them, the spear of victory, which no fight could be held against (Grey, 1983).

His epithets of Ildanach and Smildanach were given after he appeared at Tara to join the Tuatha Dé Danann and his entrance was challenged; he declared himself skilled in all arts and since no one else at Tara could match his claim he was allowed to enter (Grey, 1983).

Lugh is a prominent figure in Irish mythology appearing in many stories and the holiday of Lúnasa is named for him, although it is said to memorialize his foster-mother Tailtiu.

Macha

Maiche .i. bodb; isi in tres morrigan .i. maiche ocus bodb ocus morrigan, unde mesrad maiche .i. cenna daoine iarna nairlech, ut dixit dub ruis. Garbæ adbae innon fil. i lomrad fir maiche mes, i nagat laich liu i lles, i lluaiget mna trogain tres.

(Macha, who is a Badb, one of the three Morrigans, who are Macha and Badb and Morrigan. The harvest of Macha is men's heads after the slaughter, dark and bloody. It is a rough place to live there. Macha's harvest is a payment of a pledge, the honor of warriors gathered in forts, and the cause of women's grief after battle.)

Macha is one of the three daughters of Ernmas who is given the title of Mórríghan. She appears in both battles of Maige Tuired using battle magic and in the second battle is the only female name listed among the warriors killed fighting the Fomorians. It is said, as illustrated in the quote on the previous page, that the heads of men killed in battle are her harvest and her name, like Badhbh's, is also a word that means crow. Macha is considered a Goddess of sovereignty and battle (O hOgain, 2006). She appears in other stories including a precursor to the *Táin Bó Cúailnge* where she is the one who curses the men of Ulster and sets the stage for the events of Cu Chulain's role in the cattle raid. She is associated with crows, ravens, and horses; her name means crow, and horses appear in several of her stories in significant ways. Modern practitioners may choose to honor her at Lúnasa, because that was a time when celebrations were traditionally held at her sacred site of Emhain Macha. Offerings to her may include oats, whiskey, or pork.

Mórríoghan

...In Morrigan mórda, ba slóg-dírmach sámda.
Metrical Dindshenchas
(...The exalted Morrigan, whose ease is trooping hosts.)

The Mórríoghan (Old Irish Morrigu or Morrigan) is the pre-eminent battle Goddess of the Irish, but she is also associated with prophecy, magic, and incitement. She and her sisters, Badhbh and Macha, often appear together in the first two battles of Maige Tuired using magic to attack the enemy; they also accompany the warriors to the battlefield. The Mórríoghan alone also acts in defense of her people in the *Cath Maige Tuired* by weakening the Fomorian King Indech and promising Lugh she would act decisively in the battle (Grey, 1983). She speaks repeatedly to incite warriors to act boldly, both instigating Lugh to fight against the Fomorians and at the end of the battle encouraging the Tuatha Dé Danann to victory (Grey, 1983). She is a significant factor throughout the *Táin Bó Cúailnge*, both shaping events that bring about the cattle raid and also the course of the raid itself. Throughout the myths she takes the form of a young woman, old hag, eel, wolf, cow, crow, and raven. She has several locations in Ireland associated with her, including the cave of Cruachan where it is said she turned a woman named Odras into a river for chasing her after she stole Odras's bull (Gwynn, 1906).

A complex deity, she was later associated with phantoms and terrors, yet is one of the few Irish deities explicitly called a God in the myths and to whom we have at least one preserved prayer, from a man hoping for her help in acquiring cattle (Gulermovich Epstien, 1998). Modern Irish Polytheists may honor her for a variety of reasons; offerings can include alcohol, milk, and weapons.

Nuadha

Ré secht mbliadan Nuadat narsheng
Osin chuanairt chéibfind
Flathius ind fir chichmair chuilfind
Ria tiachtain in Hérind
Lebor Gabala Erenn
(A space of seven years noble, graceful Nuada
Over a fair-haired warrior-pack
Ruled the greatly keen, fair-tressed man
Before going to Ireland.)

His main epithet is 'Airgetlamh' (silver arm) because in the first battle of Maige Tuired he lost his arm in battle against the Fir Bolg champion Sreng, and Dian Cecht and Credne replaced it with one of silver that functioned just like a real arm. Nuadha (Old Irish Nuada or Nuoda) was king of the Tuatha Dé Danann before losing his arm, but had to abdicate afterwards; seven years later his original arm was restored and he became king again. O hOgain suggests that Nuada is the same deity as Nechtan and Elcmar (O hOgain, 2006). He suggests this based on another name for Nuada being Nuada Necht, which O hOgain believes is the earlier form of Nechtan; by this association Nuada would have been the original owner of Brugh na Boyne and would also possess the source of the Boyne, the well of Nechtan. Nuada is a complex deity who can be seen as a God of battle, war, and also justice (Gray, 1983).

If weight is given to the possible connections to Nechtan and Elcmar then he could also be seen as a God of healing and of the water, particularly rivers. The sword would be one of his symbols, as he possessed the sword that was one of the four treasures, and hawks may be associated with him. I personally have experienced the hawk as a symbol and messenger of Nuada, long before finding out the version of the story that connected him to the bird through the loss of his arm. Dogs and salmon/trout may also be associated with him. As Nechtan he would be connected to salmon through the salmon of knowledge that lived at the source of the river Boyne. Appropriate offerings would seem to be fish, and I have had success offering beer and stout, particularly Guinness.

Oghma

Now Ogma, a man well skilled in speech and in poetry, invented the Ogham. The cause of its invention, as a proof of his ingenuity...the father of Ogham is Ogma, the mother of Ogham is the hand or knife of Ogma.
The Scholar's Primer

Called 'Trenfher' (strong-man), 'Grianeces' (sun-poet), and 'Grianainech' (sun-faced), Oghma (Old Irish Ogma) was a premier warrior among the Gods and known for his eloquence

(O hOgain, 2006; Jones, n.d.). As the opening quote shows, it is said that Oghma is the creator of the alphabet known as Ogham, which has both practical and esoteric uses in mythology. Oghma is a skilled warrior and he was one of the champions of the Tuatha Dé Danann. Modern Irish Polytheists may honor Oghma both for his battle prowess and his eloquence. Those who choose to work with the Ogham for either divination or magic may also choose to honor Oghma with their efforts or pray to him for assistance.

Oengus

Aengus was the leader of them all because of...the beauty of his form and the nobility of his people. He was also called in Mac Oc (the Young Son), for his mother said: 'Young is the son who was begotten at the break of day and born betwixt it and evening.'
Heroic Romances of Ireland

Called 'Mac ind Oc', which is literally 'son of the youth', O hOgain posits that originally his epithet would have been maccan óc meaning 'the young boy' (O hOgain, 2006). Oengus is a son of the Daghdha and the Goddess Bóinne and his home is at Brugh na Bóinne, also known today as Newgrange. Oengus appears in many stories with love themes: in *Tochmarc Étaine* he is instrumental in the relationship between Midir and Etain; in The Pursuit of Diarmuid and Grainne he acts several times to aid the two fleeing lovers, and in Aisling Óenguso the God himself pursues an Otherworldly woman who spends part of her time in the form of a swan. This had led many modern Irish Polytheists to see Oengus as a deity of love and relationships and to honor him as such.

Other Deities

There are also a few deities honored who are not members of the

Tuatha Dé Danann and I would like to include two of them here as well.

Donn

Said Donn: 'I shall put under the edge of spear and of sword all that are now in Ireland, only let land be reached.' The wind made a discrimination against the ship wherein were Donn the king and Airech, two of the Sons of Mil, and the ship wherein were Bres and Buas and Buaigne, till they were drowned at the Sandhills, which are called Tighi Duinn; the grave mound of every man is there.
Lebor Gabala Erenn

There is some debate about whether the Irish have a God of the dead, but if they do it's generally agreed that it would be Donn, a king of the Milesians who died at sea when the sons of Mil were trying to take Ireland. In this sense Donn is the first ancestor, the first person to die in Ireland before it was taken by people. The place where he died, off the southwest coast of Ireland, was called Tech Duinn – Donn's House. Tech Duinn became equated in folklore with the Otherworldly land of the dead and Donn with a primal ancestor and underworld God (Jones, 2004). In the Death Tale of Conaire Donn is explicitly called the King of the Dead and a 9th century text has Donn claiming that all who die will go to him and his house (O hOgain, 2006).

Manannán mac Lir

Manannán Mac Lir...inde Scoti et Britónes eum deum maris uocauerunt...
Sanas Cormac
(Manannán Mac Lir...the Irish and British called him the God of the sea.)

Given the epithet 'mac Lir' (son of the sea), Manannan's proper name is given in the *Lebor Gabála Érenn* as Oirbsiu. Manannán was originally said to live on the Isle of Man, a place seen as near mythical in Irish stories; later his home shifted fully into the Otherworld, to Eamhain (O hOgain, 2006). The Irish described Eamhain in rich detail as a sacred place, an island held up by four silver legs or pillars, on which grew magical apples that gave the island the full name of Eamhain Abhlach, Eamhain of the Apples (O hOgain, 2006).

Other names for his domain include Mag Meall (the pleasant plain) and Tír Tairngire (the land of promise) (O hOgain, 2006). Each of these names and associations reflect the connection between Manannán's realm and the Otherworld. He was seen as the lord of the waves, to whom the ocean was like a field of solid land, as well as a master magician and God who could control the weather (O hOgain, 2006). The fish are said to be his livestock, compared to cows and sheep, and the waves themselves are called his horses; his most special horse is Enbharr, (water foam), who could run over sea as if it were solid land (O hOgain, 2006).

In Irish mythology, although he was not counted among the People of Danu in stories until the 10th century, it is Manannán who advises the Tuatha Dé Danann to take up residence in the sí, and he who assigned each new home (O hOgain, 2006).

Additionally, he gives three gifts to the Tuatha de; the féth fiadha, the feast of Goibhniu, and the pigs of Manannán (O hOgain, 2006). The féth fiadha was either a spell or cloak that allowed the person to become invisible and travel unnoticed. The feast of Goibhniu was a magical feast that kept the Gods young and living. The pigs of Manannán were immortal swine who could be killed and would return to life. Some sources suggest that it was these actions that earned him a place among the Tuatha Dé Danann. However, I believe that it is more likely that he fills a role as an outsider deity, not fully part of the People of Danu nor fully separate, but liminally placed.

Spirits

The main types of spirits that are dealt with in Irish Reconstruction are the aos sí, also called fairies in English, and the land spirits. Staying on good terms with the aos sí can be difficult,[12] but is worthwhile.

The name aos sí or daoine sí, both meaning 'people of the fairy hills', comes from the belief that these beings dwelt within the hollow hills, or that those hills served as entrances to their Otherworldly realm. The daoine sí were equally likely to be connected to Otherworldly islands, usually seen in the west, which fisherman occasionally glimpsed out on the water, but could never reach, as to the hills and mounds (McNeill, 1956). In Irish lore the Fair Folk live in the land, on the sea, and in the air, being associated with the mounds, stone circles, watery locations including the sea and bogs, caverns, and strange swirls of wind, as well as specific trees, especially lone hawthorn trees (O hOgain, 2006). Looking at this we can perhaps begin to see that the Irish concept of an Saol Eile (the Other World) is as complex as the beliefs about the people (an daoine eile – the Other people, often referred to in English as the Other Crowd) who live within it.

These Otherworldly lands are described as being fair beyond measure, beautiful, peaceful, and rich. Many mortals in tales who were taken into Fairyland did not want to leave it until a longing to see their families or old homes finally over took them. Generally, when such people did leave the fairy realm they would find that hundreds of years had passed and they themselves would die as soon as they touched mortal earth, because time moves differently in the Otherworld. The concept of the Otherworld plays a significant role in Irish cosmology.

The daoine sí are often referred to with euphemisms like Good Neighbors, Good People, Other Crowd, and Fair Folk; sometimes they are called fairies. In the older belief it was thought to be bad luck to call the daoine sí by that name (or any name using 'sí'), but interestingly this prohibition seems to be shifting to the term 'fairies', which of course was originally used as a way to avoid offending them. In modern practice many people have a strong prohibition against referring to them by any form of sí or using the word fairy, sticking instead to euphemisms (O hOgain, 2006).

In folklore the daoine sí are seen as being especially active on the quarter days, Samhain, Imbolc, Bealtaine, and Lúnasa. It was believed that on these days the fairies moved house, processing forth from one hill to another along set fairy roads and that it was quite dangerous to meet them at such times (McNeill, 1956; Evans, 1957). Samhain and Bealtaine are the strongest times of fairy influence and so are times when great care should be taken to avoid running afoul of them (O hOgain, 2006). At Bealtaine it was believed that the Fair Folk might travel abroad, appearing as a stranger at the door asking for milk or a coal from the fire; to give either would mean giving the household's luck away for the year to come (Wilde, 1887). The Fair Folk are also especially active at twilight and midnight, and the slua sí, a kind of airborne malicious fairy host, is most active at night.

The daoine sí can bless or harm people. Fairy gifts could be good and benefit people, or they could be illusions that would turn to leaves or grass at dawn. The sí gaoithe (fairy wind), which was a sign of the presence of the fairy host, could bring illness or cause injury (MacKillop, 1998). Elfshot is another well-known fairy malady, a sudden pain, cramp, or stitch caused by an invisible fairy arrow shot into the body by angered daoine sí. Elfshot might also be used against cattle, which would slowly waste away after being struck (O hOgain, 1995). In contrast though, those who were considered friends of the daoine sí were often privy to special knowledge and taught things such as healing and magic, or a musician might be given great skill (O hOgain, 2006).

The daoine sí might appear as a stranger at the door seeking to borrow something or needing milk or a coal from the fire, alone in a field or wood, or might be encountered on the road. Those brave enough to seek them out might choose to sleep on a fairy mound, knowing that the result would either be blessing or madness.

Honoring and offering to the daoine sí is – or should be – an important aspect of an Irish Polytheist practice. The Fair Folk have long been offered to and this is a practice we would do well to continue in our thoroughly modern world, rather than turning our backs on the Otherworld, which has so long existed side by side with ours. Honoring the daoine sí not only prevents ill-luck, but can also grant good luck and blessing and, more importantly, helps create a reciprocal relationship between us and the Fair Folk based on respect and friendship. Humans have a long and complex relationship with the daoine sí – as long and complex as the history of the Fair Folk themselves – and they are just as present today as they have ever been.

The Irish view of spirits of the land is complicated. There is a very blurry line between a spirit that embodies a place and a spirit that inhabits it, which can make it difficult to distinguish between the two. Adding to the complication are spirits of sovereignty, which are often described as spirits of the land; I think though that sovereignty spirits are not properly land spirits, but are a higher level of being that does not embody the spirit of a place so much as represent the power to rightly rule that place and the spirits – corporeal and non corporeal – within it. Land spirits are best understood as the spirit of a specific place, the embodiment of that location's energy or soul, if you will. Unlike some other kinds of spirits, land spirits are strongly tied to a single location or natural object, such as a tree or well, and in folklore are rarely able to leave that place or object. The other types of daoine sí are well known to move their homes and travel, even far abroad. Irish land spirits may appear in human form or as birds or animals (O Suilleabhain, 1967).

The role of land spirits in Irish folklore is difficult to study because they are not often viewed as a separate category of being, although there is a tradition of malefic spirits of place. These dangerous spirits are viewed as being bound to a location and have names like Sprid na Bearnan (spirit of the gap), Sprid na Charraig an Eidhin (spirit of Carriganine), and Sprid an Tobac (spirit of the tobacco), each with their own story (O Suilleabhain, 1967).

Because these spirits are largely malevolent it was believed they must be protected against using things including iron (a chain or black handled knife specifically), holy water, or a rooster crowing (O Suilleabhain, 1967). It is possible, though, that these represent a later Christian attitude towards these spirits, rather than an older pagan one, as priests were often called to banish the spirits of these places.

In the Irish view, land spirits are associated with a specific feature of the land. This is often a large boulder, although it can also be a tree or stream. Land spirits are able to take different forms, including human and animal and may appear as guardians of certain areas or places. Spirits of place may communicate directly with people who are able to hear or see them, often taking the form of a person or animal for this purpose, something that is supported in folklore. They may also appear in dreams or visions to people in order to communicate with them (Gundarsson, 2007).

Although daoine sí can and do travel, and may be found in unexpected places, land spirits are sedentary. The spirit of a tree, or boulder, or well, has physical limitations within this world, in my experience, because it is anchored or rooted by the physical item it belongs to. Similarly while the Other Crowd can influence people directly – stealing things, harming, blessing, or gifting – land spirits are more subtle. They influence us through our emotional states and through the wider flourishing or failure of a place. In my experience, while land spirits will accept, and even want, tangible offerings many of them seem to feed on energy from living things: happiness, creativity, love, and in some cases fear or other dark emotions. In response they nurture the energy they need.

Just as the connection between the Otherworldly Fair Folk and the land spirits is complicated, there is a longstanding and complex association between the Fair Folk and the dead, and indeed it is difficult to separate out the two groups in many cases. The dead often appear among the ranks of the daoine sí, especially the newly dead, and many stories feature someone seeing a thought-to-be-dead friend or relative in a marketplace. This is often explained by saying that the person had not actually died, but was in reality taken by the Fair Folk and a changeling left behind, which was buried in the person's name (a common ploy with new brides and other attractive young people). The connection runs deeper than this though, as the sí that the Fair Folk live in are often ancient burial mounds, such as Brugh na Boyne (Newgrange). In many fairy stories a person is believed to have died, but appears, often in a dream, to a loved one and explains that they have been taken into Fairyland and can be rescued in a certain way, usually by the living person going to a crossroads at midnight when the fairy rade will pass by and grabbing their loved one from the horse he or she is riding (O hOgain, 2006; The Ballad of Tam Lin). Many people say that the Slua sí, the fairy host of the air, are spirits of the mortal dead (McNeill, 1956).

Honoring ancestors is a part of the belief in spirits and that spirits can influence us. Our ancestors have a vested interest in our wellbeing and so are more easily motivated to intercede for us and also are more closely connected to us. In Irish folk belief we see the idea of honoring and offering to the dead especially at holidays, when they return to visit with their loved ones who are still living. Many Irish Polytheists I know have small ancestor shrines in their homes, places to remember and honor those who have come before, whether they are ancestors of blood or of spirit. Some have also revived a practice of hero-cults found in other cultures and incorporated aspects of this into their own religious practices. For example there is an increasingly common practice of honoring Cu Chulain in March and more widely of venerating him as an ancestral hero.[13]

The Immortality of the Soul

Several different Irish myths discuss the topic of the immortal soul including the story of Tuan mac Cairill in the *Lebor na hUidre*. In this story Tuan mac Cairill tells the tale of Ireland from the beginning, which he has witnessed throughout his various lives as a man, then as a stag, a wild boar, an eagle, a salmon, and then a man again. As he says in the story: 'My name is Tuan son of Carell. But once I was called Tuan son of Starn, son of Sera, and my father, Starn, was the brother of Partholan.' While this is obviously a storytelling device it may also hint at a belief in the continuity of the soul during the rebirth process.

We see similar concepts in myth with the story of Friuch and Rucht in *De Chopur in dá Muccida*, or Etain in *Tochmarc Etain*, where people pass through many forms, not all of them human. Although in these stories it is true that the people are often under spells of some sort, it still shows a belief in the continuity of the soul from one form to another, as we see the enchanted people being reborn into each new form.

Where it gets tricky, of course, is discussing where exactly the soul goes between lives. In the Irish belief it can get very complex, with many different options, often referred to as 'Islands in the West', being possible, as well as Tech Duinn. Folklore tells us that Tech Duinn is a place where the dead go, but not necessarily their final destination. Some believe that the house of Donn is where the dead go before moving on to the Otherworld (Ellis, 1987). In the 8th to 10th centuries Tech Duinn was seen as an assembly place of the dead, and a place that the dead both went to and left from (O hOgain, 2006). Besides Tech Duinn (present day Bull Rock, County Cork), Donn is also connected to Cnoc Firinne, in county Limerick, and Dumhcha, in county Clare. From stories we find in the Fairy Faith, and even depending on how we choose to view stories like that of Ossain and Naimh, a person may join the fairies (the daione sí) for example, or their spirit may otherwise wander, as Irish myth has an abundance of wandering souls to be found. Of course, these examples are largely from much later periods and seeing them in relation to, or connected to, older beliefs is purely modern supposition. It is difficult to know what the ancient Irish may have believed about where the soul went between lives, for all that we do seem to have decent evidence that they did believe in the soul's continuance.

Cosmology

We have no surviving creation myth or eschatology story in Irish Polytheism, although we can safely assume that there were originally such myths. Looking carefully at the *Lebor Gabála Érenn* we may be able to pick out hints of an older creation story, and some people have made efforts to reconstruct one from this. Additionally, several scholars and various neopagan authors have put forth versions of an Irish or Celtic creation story. The closest we come to an end-of-the-world story may be the Morrigan's second prophecy in the *Cath Maige Tuired*, which predicts a time of great trouble and disorder.

> Íarus fis, túathus cath, airthius bláth, teissius séis, fortius flaith.
> *Suidigud Tellaich Temra*
> (In the west knowledge, in the north battle, in the east blossoming, in the south melody, in the center sovereignty.)

Cosmology in Irish Polytheism is complex, but the above quote from the *Suidigud Tellaich Temra* illustrates several important aspects. The world is divided into five sections, each with its own particular qualities; the story goes on to give long, detailed lists for each direction. Not only do we see that there are five directions, but we also see the qualities that are seen as valuable. Although many modern people dislike the idea of battle, in the older Irish material boldness in battle, courage, and a willingness to fight were all seen as valuable qualities. In the same way wisdom, blossoming – or productivity and flourishing – skill with music, and sovereignty, are all important qualities – both to the individual and in a wider cosmological sense.

We are told in the Cauldron of Poesy that each person is born with three energetic cauldrons within them. The three are: the cauldron of incubation, the cauldron of motion, and the cauldron of wisdom (Laurie, 1996). The state of each cauldron affects a person's health and wisdom and is in turn affected by their actions. Additionally, the head was believed to be the seat of the soul and the container of personal power (O hOgain, 1999). There is a concept of the dúile, the elements, which vary in number in the source material, but are often perceived as nine by Reconstructionists. They relate not only to different natural things, but also correspond to different parts of the human body (O'Dubhain, 1997).

It can generally be said that rivers were seen as channels of energy from the Otherworld and associated with specific Goddesses (O hOgan, 2006). In the same way looking at mythology makes it clear that sovereignty belonged to Goddesses who chose kings to bestow this right to rule upon. Whereas the deities of the Tuatha Dé Danann represented order and civilization, the beings they contested with, such as the Fir Bolg and Fomorians, represented entropy and chaos (O hOgain, 2006). This underscores another basic cosmological principle, that of fírinne, or truth, as a force that acts within all things. To live in right relation to fírinne is to live in right relation with the proper order of the world and to flourish, while to live against fírinne is to live outside right order and to invite chaos. This core principle is expressed in several wisdom texts including the *Audacht Morainn* and the *Tecosca Cormaic*. Moderation is also strongly emphasized in both texts as a way to live in fírinne, finding a balance between too much and too little of anything.

There is an emphasis on moving sunwise for blessing and counterclockwise for baneful reasons (McNeil, 1956). In modern Irish folk belief sacred sites are circled three times sunwise before being entered (Evans, 1957). For an Irish Polytheist today it is important to continue this practice and to understand the significance of the directions we move in.

Chapter 3

How Do We Do It?

Bennacht nime, nél-bennacht,
Bennacht tíre, torad-bennacht,
Bennacht mara, íasc-bennacht.
(Blessing of sky, cloud-blessing
Blessing of earth, produce-blessing
Blessing of sea, fish-blessing.)

Ritual

We have no historic examples of complete pagan rituals. What we do have are hints and pieces of things that can be used in a modern context for rituals and an idea of what a basic Irish pagan ritual structure would have been.

Now, as an Irish Polytheist, when I do rituals it's usually just me, or me and my children. This is just a basic outline for home rituals, and this is only the way that I do things although it reflects my understanding of Reconstructionist-style ritual and some general principles behind the ritual style I use. I'm not trying to put this out there as any sort of set ritual format for anyone but myself. As with so many aspects of Irish Reconstruction and Irish Polytheism more generally there will be variations in how people do certain things and why.

At its most basic, rituals follow a simple outline of creating or acknowledging sacred space, invoking the Powers to be honored, making offerings, acknowledging the reason for the ritual, offering, giving thanks, divination, and feasting. Acknowledging the sacredness of the ritual space is a good way to begin, and I generally do this by burning an herb traditionally associated with blessing. Invocation is traditional and can be found in prayers and rituals throughout the ancient world. Offerings are usually made either into water or fire. In Ireland, water was a well-known place to deposit offerings, with many votive deposits found in lakes and bogs; the items are generally broken first as a token that they belong fully to the Otherworld after being given (O hOgain, 1999). I usually make offerings twice in my rituals – once after invoking the deity or deities I am honoring and again after discussing the reason for the ritual and usually giving a prayer or chant. After the second offering I give thanks to the Powers being honored[14] and will usually use some form of divination to see if the period until the next ritual looks propitious. Afterwards, feasting is traditional, with some portion of the food given to the Gods and spirits.

In my personal rituals I start off by burning juniper, vervain, or an incense blend I make that combines several herbs and woods used historically for cleansing. I walk three times sunwise around my ritual space, sometimes carrying the incense. After this I acknowledge the ancestors, the daoine sidhe, the Gods. If a specific holy day or occasion is associated with one or two deities then I will only call that one or those two when calling the Gods. I invoke[15] each Power and make offerings to them appropriate to their nature and which are environmentally safe. For example, I might offer incense made from organic local plants, I might light a candle, I might write a poem and then burn the only copy during ritual, I might burn butter or olive oil, I might pour out pure water, milk, cream, or alcohol. After all the guests have been invited to the party, so to speak, I will talk a little about the purpose of the rite, perhaps read a poem or blessing – often something traditional from a mythology, sometimes modernized or made pagan if necessary. If I know any appropriate songs I would sing them now. Some specific holy days such as Bealtaine or Samhain have particular actions or activities that might occur, while others are more general. This is when any special activity or prayers would be done, followed by divination to assess the luck of the coming days. The gathered Powers are acknowledged and thanked for their presence. The energy of the ritual is grounded as an offering to the earth, and any physical offerings that weren't burned are given to a pit in the earth or to a swamp behind my house. Usually this is followed by feasting with food chosen to fit the theme of the ritual.

Offerings

Offerings to the daoine sí traditionally include milk, butter, and bread, left by the doorway or at the roots of a fairy tree, as well as a bit of whatever one is drinking poured out onto the ground (Evans, 1957). Additionally, milk might sometimes be thrown in the air for the fairies or butter buried near a bog as an offering to them (O hOgain, 1995). At holy days it was also a custom to offer a heavy porridge that might be poured into a hole in the earth, or bread could be left out or tossed over the shoulder (McNeill, 1956; Sjoedstedt, 2000). The custom of pouring a drink out is mentioned in *Irish Folk Ways*, and is something I was familiar with as a family custom; my grandfather would pour out a bit of his beer in this manner, and while my father didn't, that I know of, I've long been in the habit myself of offering a portion of anything I am drinking outdoors to the Good People. In a modern context people seem to offer milk, cream, bread or other baked goods, honey, and portions of meals, as well as alcohol.

Offering to the ancestors traditionally include a portion of meals being eaten by the family, clean water, or the lighting of a white candle (Danaher, 1972). In a modern context many people also choose to offer things that the person would have enjoyed in life, such as coffee or tea. Offerings of drinks may be left on the ancestor shrine, if you have one, or poured out onto the earth.

Offerings to the Gods can be tailored to each deity based on their mythology or personal preference. We can also look at archaeology and folklore to guide our choices. Votive deposits in lakes usually included jewelry and weapons (O hOgain, 1999).

Archaeology shows animal offerings of cows and pigs primarily (McCormick, 2010). From this we could extrapolate that offerings of cooked beef or pork would be acceptable to most deities, or could be featured as the focus of after ritual feasting to be shared with the Gods. Given the preference for milk and bread as offerings, and their mention specifically in the *De Gabáil in t-Sída*, either of those would also make a good choice as well.

Daily Practices

Daily practices in Irish Polytheism will vary greatly from person to person. Some people may not feel the need to use any daily practices and stay with seasonal ritual observations, while others may have involved daily practices. Some daily practices may include prayers, small offerings, and devotional study. Offerings have already been discussed and devotional study is simply the study of a specific subject as an act of devotion – perhaps learning Irish for example – but prayers may be the most common. There are a wide array of traditional daily prayers that can be used from Irish mythology and folklore.

One example of a daily prayer that seems to be common among Irish Polytheists is called the Deer's Cry, or Fáed Fíada. The Fáed Fíada is a portion of Saint Patrick's Lorica and is said to be much older and reflect a pagan prayer. I've always liked and have based one of my own daily prayers on the style of it.

Fáed Fíada
Atomriug indiu
niurt nime,
soilsi gréne,
étrochtai éscai,
áni thened,
déni lóchet,
luaithi gaíthe,
fudomnai mara,

tairismigi thalman,
cobsaidi ailech.[16]
(I bind today
strength of sky
light of sun
radiance of moon
brightness of flame
swiftness of light
speed of wind
depth of ocean
steadfastness of earth
firmness of rock.)

Altars and Shrines

We have very little surviving information on Irish pagan altars.
We can look at early Christian shrines and altars, Neolithic stone
altars, and what little information we do have in myths. Modern
Irish Polytheists may choose not to have any permanent altar or
may choose to use a small stone structure outdoors, or find a
small grove of trees. Another option would be to use one's own
inspiration to create a small space for use during rituals.
Ultimately, the purpose of an altar, like a ritual itself, is simply to
create a place of connection with the divine, a place to make
offerings, and to pray or make petitions. This being the case it is
really up to the person to find out what works best for them in
their unique circumstances. Historically, the daoine sí were
offered to both in the home and at sites associated with them,
which could include hills or trees. Ancestors might have offerings
left for them at their graves or in the home, usually the kitchen (O
hOgain, 1999; Danaher, 1972). Offerings for the Gods, as briefly
mentioned before, might be left in pits, in water, or burned. This
being the case offerings are only left on altars temporarily before
being removed, with the Powers taking the substance of the
offering and leaving behind the physical form. This concept is

discussed, especially in relation to the daoine si in books such as *The Fairy Faith in Celtic Countries,* but can be extrapolated out to the Gods and ancestors as well.

Generally my approach to an ancestor altar is to set up a small space with pictures or tokens of those I am honoring. For the daoine sí it is best to try to find a tree, large rock, or natural site that you can feel their presence, but a small space may be set up in the home as well. For the Gods I like to keep an area with images of the Gods my household honors where I can burn candles and leave offerings as well as pray.

Some Celtic pagans prefer not to use images of the Gods, following the idea that the Celts themselves did not do so. A main source for this belief is a quote from the Gaulish chieftain Brennus, who sacked Rome and was said to have been incredulous at the idea of statues of the Gods in human form in temples:

> Brennus, the king of the Gauls, on entering a temple found no dedications of gold or silver, and when he came only upon images of stone and wood he laughed at them, to think that men, believing that gods have human form, should set up their images in wood and stone.
> (Diodorus Siculus)

From a purely Irish perspective there is limited evidence. There are many natural locations and features that are associated with the various Irish Gods, but actual man-made representations do not seem to be major features in the archaeological records. We have anecdotal evidence in the folklore that the Gods were believed to take human form and appear to people or possibly even interact in our world. The conception of Cu Chulain, for example, where Lugh appears to Deichtine and the men of Ulster or the story of Macha marrying the peasant Crunnchu. O hOgain quotes Dillion' Serglige Con Culainn, saying: 'He states that they [the Tuatha Dé Danann] 'used to fight men in bodily form...'" (O hOgain, 1999, p 213). This supports the idea that the Irish did anthropomorphize their Gods, a key requirement for depicting Gods in statuary. We also have some evidence, albeit less persuasive, of the use of imagery through the story of Crom Cruach (or Cenn Cruach) who was said to have a stone or gold idol at Mag Slecht surrounded by 12 smaller stone statues (O hOgain, 2006).

We may conclude that the Irish saw their Gods as living beings who could appear to people, and perhaps had no need, therefore, to depict them in imagery. We can also say that there did not appear to be any prohibition against it and that there were many examples of a type of idolatry using symbolic representations such as stones or places believed to belong to that Power. In the wider Celtic world, including Wales and England, we do find statuary used, so the choice to use or not use statuary by Irish Polytheists should be entirely personal, as either would be historically supported.

For myself I enjoy using statuary. I like having something in ritual to represent the deity I am trying to connect to and I believe that it helps me focus in prayer. I like to find a statue that really resonates with me and then I paint it myself. Sometimes the statue that I feel most represents a deity I honor isn't supposed to be that deity, but I'll use it anyway if it works for me. I feel that the painting really helps connect it to that deity and to get some of myself into it.

Chapter 4

What Are the Holy Days?

The main holidays generally celebrated by Irish Polytheists are Samhain, Imbolc, Bealtaine, and Lúnasa; some people also acknowledge the solar festivals, but the four fire festivals are the most commonly celebrated by all. Despite this apparent universal acknowledgement of these holidays there is a variance in how people date them; probably the single most consistent debate you can count on seeing in the Celtic pagan community is about the dating of the four fire festivals. Like all such debates, each side tends to hold its own view quite passionately. There are three main arguments: the dates of the celebrations were set astronomically; the dates were set using a calendar; the dates were based on agricultural signs. Each side has merit, but the truth is there is not enough solid evidence to ever know with certainty how the ancients timed their celebrations.

The astrology argument is based on setting the dates exactly midway between the solstices and equinoxes. This usually puts them roughly six weeks after one solar holiday and six weeks before the next solar holiday, so that Samhain for example, is about six weeks after the fall equinox and six weeks before the winter solstice. In some cases people suggest using a specific marker such as a constellation being at a certain point in the sky or a sign of the zodiac at a certain degree. The ancient stone circles and mounds that are aligned with certain times are also used, so that when the light of the sun hits a certain point or illuminates the interior of the mound it would indicate that the holiday should be celebrated. This argument naturally hinges on two premises: that the ancients celebrated the solar holidays as well, and that they were aware of the alignments of the ancient Neolithic monuments. There is also a related argument that uses lunar dating, based from what I have seen on the second full moon after the solar event.[17]

The calendar argument dates the celebration on the first day of the respective months they occur on: February, May, August, and November. We have references in the mythology dating back to the 11th century of Lúnasa, Bealtaine, and Samhain being on the 'kalends'[18] (first day) of those months and we know historically they were celebrated on those days in folk practice. This is somewhat complicated by the fact that the calendar system switched from the Julian to the Gregorian and when that occurred the dates shifted. When the calendar shift occurred in the UK in 1752 it moved everything back 11 days, meaning what was the first of November is now the 12th. Even a hundred years ago in several areas people were still celebrating Imbolc and Lúnasa in particular on the 12th of February and August respectively because they were using the old dating. What this means in practice is that when we see older references to the days being celebrated on the first of the month we need to understand that they are equivalent for us today to the 12th of that same month. A Irish Reconstructionist who wanted to use the calendar dates could, I think, choose to either go by the first of the month still or use the older dating and celebrate on the 12th.

The final method of dating the celebration of the holiday is based on observation of agricultural markers and the idea that each holiday is agrarian at heart and depends on certain conditions being met. Imbolc is a celebration of the return of fresh milk and would be celebrated when the lambs were born or the sheep came into milk. Bealtaine is the beginning of summer, a time when the herds are moved to summer pastures, and would have been celebrated when the people were confident winter had passed; this is often said to be marked by the blooming of the hawthorn and indeed many Bealtaine traditions require flowers. Lúnasa was the beginning of the harvest – nothing could be harvested before the proper time by longstanding tradition – and of the harvest fairs. It would have been celebrated when the grain crops were ready to be gathered.

Samhain was the beginning of winter, when the herds were brought back in from the summer pastures and extra stock was butchered. It also marked the end of the harvest and gathering anything after Samhain was prohibited as everything left belonged to the daoine sí. Many people say that Samhain would have been celebrated after the first hard frost; there is a certain logic to this as frost would ruin any crops left in the fields.[19] This method of dating is the least rigid and most changeable of the three, and also can prove difficult for people who are far removed from the farming cycle.

Each of these approaches has merit, and each has problems. No one is a perfect solution or can be proven beyond question to be the historical method. It is up to individuals to decide which method they prefer and learn how best to apply it within their own practice.

Samhain

I shall fight without harm to myself from Samuin, i.e., the end of summer. For two divisions were formerly on the year, viz., summer from Beltaine (the first of May), and winter from Samuin to Beltaine. Or sainfuin, viz., suain (sounds), for it is then that gentle voices sound, viz., sám-son 'gentle sound'.
Wooing of Emer

With the men of Ireland too it was general that out of all airts they should resort to Tara in order to the holding of Tara's Feast at samhaintide. For these were the two principal gatherings that they had: Tara's Feast at every samhain (that being the heathens' Easter); and at each Lúnasa, or 'Lammas-tide', the Convention of Taillte.
The Birth of Aedh Slaine

Samhain has a wide array of folk traditions associated with it, as well as few hints of practices from mythology. Usually a three-day celebration, fires are extinguished and re-lit from one central sacred fire. The spirits of the dead are believed to return to their homes on Samhain and it is a folk practice to leave out a plate of food, a glass of water, or to light a white candle to welcome them (Danaher, 1972). Additionally, it is believed that Samhain is a time when the aos sí are very active and great care must be taken not to run afoul of them.

Samhain was the turning point from summer to winter and the leading theory is that the word Samhain means 'summer's end' although the etymology is uncertain. In practice, Samhain celebrations occurred in November because this was the end of the harvest and the time when the herds were brought back in from the fields, but it wasn't until the Catholic church moved its celebration of All Saints and All Souls day to the first days of November that Samhain seem to have gotten a set calendar date in a modern context (Evans, 1957; McNeill, 1961). Of course then the switch was made from the Julian to Gregorian calendar and so you still see people celebrating Samhain on November 12th, refusing to acknowledge the change (McNeill, 1961). Caesar said the Celts started the new day at sunset and the new year at Samhain, so people often choose to begin celebrating a holiday at sunset the night before the calendar date. In Irish belief, it was actually on November 2nd that the spirits of the dead returned to visit the living (Freeman, 2002; Danaher, 1972). This might support Samhain as a three-day celebration.

It was an old practice in Ireland to light a candle for each deceased member of the family and to leave the doors unlocked – in some cases even open – and to leave out either fresh water or porridge as an offering to those ancestors who chose to visit (Evans, 1957; Danaher, 1972). Additionally, Samhain was associated with a solar cross charm similar to the Brighid's cross of Imbolc and with using fire to bless the property (Danaher,

1972; McNeill 1962). Both of these practices can be continued today.

The following is a prayer in Old Irish (with the translation) which I personally use every year at Samhain:

Scél lemm dúib:
Dordaid dam,
Snigid gaim,
Ro-fáith sam;
Gáeth ard úar,
Ísel grían,
Gair a rith,
Ruirthech rían;
Ro-rúad rath
Ro-cleth cruth,
Ro-gab gnáth
Guigrann guth;
Ro-gab úacht
Etti én
Aigre re
É mo scél.
(News for you
Hear the stag's cry
Snows of winter
Summer has gone
Wind high, cold,
Low the sun,
Short his track
Heavy sea
Deep-red ferns
Lost their shape
Wild goose cries
A usual cry
Takes hold the cold

On birds' wings
An ice time
This my news)

Imbolc

To Oimolc, i.e., the beginning of spring, viz., different (ime) is its wet (folc), viz the wet of spring, and the wet of winter. Or, oi-melc, viz., oi, in the language of poetry, is a name for sheep, whence oibá (sheep's death) is named, ut dicitur coinbá (dog's death), echbá (horse's death), duineba (men's death), as bath is a name for 'death'. Oi-melc, then, is the time in which the sheep come out and are milked, whence oisc (a ewe), i.e., oisc viz., barren sheep.
Wooing of Emer

Of the four fire festivals, Imbolc (called Oimelc in Old Irish) is the most focused on the family. Celebrated on February 1st if you are going by the calendar date the celebration of Imbolc truly begins the evening before. We have no surviving information about ancient practices with this holiday, but we do have an abundance of modern folk practices.

In most parts of Ireland the women of the household, especially the oldest daughter, played the most important role during this holiday, which honored the Goddess Brighid. One practice that was common in the north and west of Ireland was for the oldest daughter to take on the role of the Goddess and to arrive at the door with the reeds to weave new Brighid's crosses, symbols of health, blessing, and protection, which were freshly woven each year (Danaher, 1972). The girl would knock three times on the door announcing her presence as Brighid. The family would welcome her in, after which they would sit down to a large meal of dairy products and, if they could afford it, mutton (Danaher, 1972).

Another popular tradition was the creation of a brideog, a

small doll or effigy representing the Goddess. A brideog could be made from a repurposed child's doll, the dash from a butter churn, leftover rushes from weaving the crosses, or the last sheaf of wheat from the previous year's harvest. The doll would be dressed in white or otherwise decorated with crystals or shells (Danaher, 1972; Carmichael, 1900). In some areas of Ireland the doll would be taken by the girls and carried from door to door in the village, pronouncing blessing on each home while the girls in turn received donations of food (Danaher, 1972). In other places the brideog would be taken outside and welcomed in, then taken to a bed that had been prepared next to the hearth and a white wand placed in with her; in the morning if the sign of the wand or footprints were seen in the ashes it was considered a very good omen (Carmichael, 1900).

Divination on this holiday begins with checking the ashes for marks. If none are found a chicken is taken to a three-way crossroads and buried and incense is burned in hope of appeasing Brighid (Carmichael, 1900). In a modern context incense can still be used, but alternative offerings, perhaps of dairy products can be made instead to regain the Goddess's favor.

The weather on Imbolc is also thought to be pretentious:

As far as the wind shall enter the door
On the Feast Day of Bride,
The snow shall enter the door
On the Feast Day of Patrick.
(*Carmina Gadelica*, 1900)

Although Imbolc occurred during the winter period of the year it was a time to look forward to the coming summer. The return of fresh dairy was celebrated, and this food featured prominently in feasts and offerings. It was also a time to bless the household and invite in the presence of the Goddess Brighid, who has been discussed previously. A family or individual desiring to celebrate

Imbolc has many traditions to work with.[20]

Bealtaine

To Beldine, i.e. Beltine, viz., a favouring fire. For the druids used to make two fires with great incantations, and to drive the cattle between them against the plagues, every year. Or to Beldin, viz., Bel the name of an idol. At that time the young of every neat were placed in the possession of Bel. Beldine, then Beltine.
Wooing of Emer,

Belltaine .i. bil tene .i. tene śoinmech .i. dáthene dognítis druidhe tria thaircedlu...móraib combertis na cethrai arthedmannaib cacha bliadna cusnaténdtibsin
MARG-L eictis na cethra etarru
(Bealtaine, meaning lucky fire or fire of abundance, a festival with two fires made by Druidic incantations...made for the young herds to receive blessing every year against illnesses [note – the herds need to be driven between the fires])[21]

Like Samhain, Bealtaine was a three-day celebration that had many folk practices associated with it. The fire was extinguished and re-lit, also echoing Samhain and, as we see in the quote from the *Sanas Cormac* above, it was an old practice to build two fires and drive livestock between them for blessing. Herbs and dew were gathered on Bealtaine morning and water from holy wells was taken at dawn with the belief that it held a special potency. The fairies were especially active and there were strong prohibitions about lending out fire or milk to strangers lest they be fairies in disguise and steal the families luck.

In Ireland up to fairly recent times, bonfires were a large public affair that occurred the night before or on the night of Bealtaine, and were true bonfires, or 'bone-fires', made with the bones of cows and horses, the horns of cows, and wood (Evans, 1957). According to the oldest stories and myths during the pagan period all the home fires would be put out and relit from a great central fire kindled by the Druids on Bealtaine morning. In modern practice the bonfires would be jumped over as a show of courage and to increase fertility (Evans, 1957).

On May Day morning a branch of rowan might be woven into the ceiling to protect the house and all within it for the next year, as rowan was thought to be an ideal protection against enchantments (Danaher, 1972). One ceremony noted from Laois Ireland called for the head of the family to light a candle and bless the door, hearth, and the four corners of the home, as well as each family member from oldest to youngest, and then the area around the home where a rowan branch should be placed. (Danaher, 1972). Many of these traditions are rooted in the belief that on Bealtaine the aos sí are particularly active and likely to be out causing mischief. One of the Fair Folk might appear at a family's door asking to borrow some milk or a coal from the fire and if any was lent out the family's luck for the year would be lost (Wilde, 1991).

In Ireland, it has been the custom for the children to gather flowers on May eve, possibly a holdover of the people once going out before dawn on May morning; these flowers were then hung up or strewn around the home for luck (Danaher, 1972). On May Day itself, flowers were tied to the bridles of horses and the horns of cows for the same purpose (Danaher, 1972). Flowers were also gathered and used to decorate wells, in order to bless and protect them (Evans, 1957).

Another custom was the preparation of a female effigy, called the 'May Baby' that was bedecked with flowers and paraded around the town or village; some theorize that this is an older pagan element related to honoring a Goddess (Danaher, 1972). A related practice was the May Boys, a troupe of boys or young men that traveled around singing songs such as:

Summer! Summer! The milk of the heifers,
And ourselves brought the summer with us,
The yellow summer, the white daisy,
And ourselves brought the summer with us!

A widespread tradition was the placement of a 'May bush', a branch or bough of a tree (sometimes hawthorn or holly) that was placed by the front door for luck and decorated with yellow flowers, brightly colored ribbons, and egg shells (Danaher, 1972). On the night of May Day candles might be lit on or around the bush and people would gather and dance around it; in Ireland in previous centuries large parties were held which included feasting and music (Danaher, 1972). The bush itself might be left standing all month, or until the decorations began falling apart, or in some areas was burned in the night-time bonfire (Danaher, 1972).

In Ireland divination on Bealtaine focused largely on the weather for the coming growing season. The direction that the wind was blowing on Bealtaine day would indicate whether the summer would be a good one or a bad one, and in some areas snow still visible on Bealtaine was seen as a very bad omen (Danaher, 1972). Another Irish practice was to sweep the threshold clean and then lightly scatter ashes over it; in the morning a footprint coming into the home meant a marriage, while one leaving meant a death in the family in the coming year (Wilde, 1991).

Lúnasa

Co ndénta a cluiche cacha bliadna ic Lug .i. Coícthiges ria lugnasad & coicthiges iar lugnasad. Lugnasad .i. noasad Loga meic Eithnend ainm in chluiche.
Lebor Gabala Erenn

•

(With a festival every year at Lúnasa, that is 15 days before Lúnasa and 15 days after Lúnasa. Lúnasa, that is a death commemoration Lugh son of Eithne named the festival.)

To Brón Trogaill, i.e. Lammas-day, viz., the beginning of autumn; for it is then the earth is afflicted, viz., the earth under fruit. Trogam is a name for 'earth'.
Wooing of Emer

...and at each Lúnasa, or 'Lammas-tide', the Convention of Taillte. All precepts and all enactments which in either of these festivals were ordained by the men of Ireland, during the whole space of that year none might infringe.
Silva Gadelica

Lúnasa[22] was once a holiday celebrated over several weeks, beginning most likely on or around August 1st. The most well known Irish name of the festival, Lúghnasa or Lúnasa, can be broken down into Lugh Nasadh and translated into either Middle or Old Irish as the assembly of Lugh or the funeral assembly of Lugh. The connection to a funeral assembly undoubtedly references the belief that the celebration was originally created by Lugh as a memorial for his foster mother, Tailtiu, after her death, and the assembly of Lugh is thought to refer to the many athletic games and competitions associated with the harvest fairs that occurred at this time.

The other Irish name, Brón Trogain, is usually understood to mean 'earth's sorrow', with the implication of the weight of the harvest, and is seen as a metaphor for birth (MacNeill, 1962). Brón means sorrow, grief, burden, or lamentation; Trogain means earth and autumn. (eDIL, n.d.). MacNeill suggests, based on passages from the *Acallamh na Senórach*, that Brón Trogain was the older name for the holiday, which only later came to be known as Lúnasa.

There are several themes surrounding this celebration that include the mundane, the spiritual, and the blending of both. Lúnasa celebrates, at its core, the beginning of the harvest and the new abundance of food being gathered; because of this it is strongly associated with the cooking of specific foods that represented the harvest, especially porridge and bread, often with fresh seasonal fruit being incorporated (Danaher, 1972). There is also mention of cows being milked in the morning and the milk used in the feast, as well as a special type of bread being made from harvested grain and cooked with rowan or another sacred wood before being handed out by the head of the household to the family who eats it and then walks sun-wise around the cooking fire, chanting a blessing prayer (McNeill, 1959).

It was understood that the period just prior to the beginning of the harvest was the leanest of the year, making the celebration of fresh fruit, vegetables, and grains all the more special to the people (MacNeill, 1962). This may also be symbolically related to another legend of Lúnasa, the battle between the God Lugh and the mysterious mythic figure of Crom Dubh. Crom Dubh means the 'black bent one' and he had a special day on the last Sunday of July called Domhnach Crom Dubh and a dangerous bull bent on destruction that had to be stopped to preserve the harvest (Kondratiev, 1998). Many of the myths relating to Lugh and Crom Dubh, who is sometimes called Crom Cruach, involve Lugh battling and outwitting Crom and thus insuring the safety and bounty of the harvest; in some cases this theme is given the additional layer of the defeat, sacrifice, consumption, and then resurrection of Crom's bull, which may argue for an older element of bull sacrifice on this day (MacNeill, 1962). The *Carmina Gadelica* records several specific actions and charms to be done during the first harvest which expand on the importance of this turning point of the year.

Another common practice at Lúnasa was for people to gather together outdoors at a traditional place, often with the entire community getting together, and the site chosen would not only be someplace beautiful and wild, but also remote enough that travelling to it would represent something of a challenge (Danaher, 1972).

Other practices of Lúnasa include decorating holy wells and pillar stones on this date, and also of travelling to hill or mountaintops; all of these varied by location and indicate that while the festival itself was widespread the nature of the celebration was dependent on the area and took on a unique local flavor (MacNeill, 1962). There are references to blessing cattle on the eve of Lúnasa and of making blessing charms for the cattle and milking equipment that the blessing would remain for the year to come (McNeill, 1959).

Divination was practiced, with a particular focus on the weather during the harvest and this seems to have been based on observations of the weather so far during the year and on atmospheric conditions on Lúnasa, with color and appearance of certain landmarks indicating either fair or foul weather to come (Danaher, 1972).

Lúnasa was also the time in Ireland, Scotland, and the Orkneys for handfastings and weddings, or the dissolution of unions formed in the previous year (McNeill, 1959). Trial marriages of this type were used to see if the new couple was compatible; should they choose to separate after a year there was no shame in it and any child that was produced from the union would be ranked with the father's legal heirs (McNeill, 1959). Finally, Lúnasa was also well known for harvest fairs and an assortment of athletic competitions and horse races; it is important to note that the ancient fairs, or oenacha, were not occasions of commerce, but of social gathering and celebration (MacNeill, 1962). Many different types of games were held, as well as competitions of agility and strength, fire leaping, and swimming races of both men and horses (Danaher, 1972). A general party atmosphere prevailed with dancing and music, storytelling, feasting, and bonfires (Hopman, 2008).

Overall it can be gathered from a wide understanding of the various Lúnasa customs that this celebration was one based on the gathering together of the community to celebrate the fresh abundance of a new harvest with joy and enjoyment. People gathered to reinforce and celebrate the bonds of community through marriages and social mixing, and to strengthen and honor the bonds between the people and the spirits of the land and the Gods through decorating wells and standing stones, the retelling or re-enactment of mythological tales, acts of blessing, and ritual.

It is unknown now exactly what pagan religious ceremonies may have been held on Lúnasa, but there are several deities that we do know are associated with this holy day. The most obvious deity associated with Lúnasa is of course Lugh, who battles with Crom Dubh and is also said to have instituted the games to commemorate his foster mother. Tailtiu herself could be another deity associated with Lúnasa, as could the Goddess Áine, who in some mythology is connected to both a three-day period during Lúnasa and to the mythic figure of Crom Dubh as his consort during this time (MacNeill, 1962).

Another Goddess associated with Lúnasa is Macha, one of the Morrioghans, who some believe raced the king's horses on Lúnasa; whether or not this is so, there is evidence of a longstanding celebration of Lúnasa at Emain Macha and the surrounding areas in Ulster (MacNeill, 1962).

Chapter 5

Magic and Mysticism

From a historic perspective both mythology and comments made by Greek and Roman authors support the importance of magical practices to the ancient Celts. Beyond that, when we look at the ancient pagan world we see magic everywhere, from daily household protection charms to spells to curse or subdue an enemy. This magic seems to have been so integral to people's lives that even after converting from paganism much of the magic survived in folk practice. We can see a multitude of examples of this in the *Carmina Gadelica* as well as different books looking at Irish folk belief such as Lady Wilde's *Ancient Irish Charms and Superstitions*.

From what I've gathered in my studies, magic was a utilitarian tool that was applied to anything and everything by those who used it. Like any tool one had to know how to use it, but there did not seem to be any idea of reserving the little magics for extreme situations. One of my favorite examples of this is a curse tablet found at the site of Sulis's shrine in Bath where the writer asks that a curse be placed on whoever stole his cloak. When we look at the charms and spells in the *Carmina Gadelica* we see folk magic for a variety of life issues, from protecting cattle to getting butter to churn properly. From this observation I've come to approach magic in the same way, as a useful tool that can and should be used to help in my life. Rather like indoor plumbing, if it's there why not use it? The same rules apply to using magic as would apply to using a physical object, that is using it properly, cautiously, and with an understanding of its effects. Magic in Reconstructionism is not ubiquitous, however, and some people reject its use entirely.

Whether or not one chooses to incorporate the practice of

magic into one's reconstruction of Irish Polytheism is an entirely personal decision. Since it is a significant historical practice, I feel it's important to include a chapter on it in this book, and specifically discuss the way Reconstructionism approaches and handles the use of folk magic and traditional magical practices.

To me magic is intrinsic in every aspect of my life. I can't imagine life without magic, or even Irish Polytheism for that matter. I say a blessing charm over every meal I cook, whisper protective prayers over my children before they leave the house, and give my family medicine along with healing spells when they are sick. There are also the greater magics when needed – the fith fath, the Druid mist, and such – but it's these little daily magics that are part of my life morning and night. If my life is a song that I am singing as I go, then magic is the constant tide of breathing that underlies each verse and chorus. And I wouldn't want it any other way.

I often hear Celtic Reconstructionists saying that Irish Polytheists today do not do magic, or that if we do it is not truly magic, but a kind of positive thinking or aligning with nature. I find the pervasiveness of this thought interesting, especially as the ancient Celts in myth and legend were well known to wield magic of all sorts. Certainly the practice of magic is no longer as common in Irish Polytheism as it was in the ancient world, or even one may conjecture in the past hundred years of folk practice. We do, however, have a very rich history of its use to draw on.

Historically, we know that the ancient Irish had many distinct types of magic workers, of which Druids and witches were only two. Generally, and in broad terms, witches were those who worked baneful magic; the word for witch in Irish, bantúathaid, is related to the word túath in its meaning of wicked or perverse, going against the right order. Druids were known to be supporters of the right order and community. Additionally we see corrguine (modern Irish asarlaí), sorcerers, mentioned and later terms like badb as a title for baneful witches. The use of magic in an Irish context was clearly complex and nuanced.

The Tuatha Dé Danann had sorcerers (corrguinigh), Druids (Draoi), and witches (draíodóir) who did magic for them in the battle against the Fomorians and looking at what the *Cath Maige Tuired* tells us about what each group brings to the fight is enlightening.

'Os sibsie, a corrgunechai', al Lugh, 'cia cumang?'
'Ni anse', ar na corrguinigh, 'a mbuind banai forra iarna trascrad trienar cerd-ne, goro marbtar a n-aiscid,, ocus da trian a neirt do gaid foraib, lie forgabail aru fual.'
('And ye, O sorcerers', saith Lugh, 'what power will ye wield?'
'Not hard to say,' quoth the sorcerers. 'Their white soles on them when they have been overthrown by our craft, till their heroes are slain, and to deprive them of two thirds of their might, with constraint on their urine.')
(Stokes, 1926)

The sorcerers are using a specific type of battle magic, which we also see the three Mórríoghans using. This particular power is used to weaken an enemy by taking 'two-thirds' of their strength from them, allowing them to be more easily overcome. Interestingly, we are also told that the sorcerers will bind the enemy warriors' urine so that they cannot relieve themselves.

'Os sib-sie, a druíde,' ol Luog, 'cía cumong?'
'Ní anse,' ar na druíde. 'Dobérom-ne cetha tened fo gnúisib no Fomore gonar'fétad fégodh a n-ardou, corus-gonot fou cumas iond óicc bet ag imgoin friu.'
('And you, Druids,' said Lug, 'what power?'
'Not hard to say,' said the Druids. 'We will bring showers of fire upon the faces of the Fomoire so that they cannot look

up, and the warriors contending with them can use their force to kill them.')

(Stokes, 1926)

The Druids in this case brought rosc catha (battle magic), something we also see attributed to the Mórríoghans. In other myths we see Druids using wands to enchant people by changing their shape and to divine the truth of a situation. We know that they were said to use spoken magic to call up ceo draiodheachte (the druidic mist), and the feth fiada (a spell of invisibility). Druids could influence the weather, divine the future and the truth of the present, bless, curse, and create illusions.

'Os siuh-sie, a Bhé Culde & a Dinand,' or Lug fria dá bantúathaid, 'cía cumang connai isin cath?'

'Ní anse,' ol síed. 'Dolbfamid-ne na cradnai & na clochai ocus fódai an talmon gommod slúag fon airmgaisciud dóib; co rainfed hi techedh frie húatbás & craidenus.'

(Stokes, 1926)

('And you, Bé Chuille and Díanann,' said Lug to his two witches, 'what can you do in the battle?'

'Not hard to say,' they said. 'We will enchant the trees and the stones and the sods of the earth so that they will be a host under arms against them; and they will scatter in flight terrified and trembling.')

As we can see, each brought a different power or skill to the battle. The witches bring the ability to enchant the earth against the enemy to create fear. While the first two types of magic users are clearly using battle magic, the witches' magic is more subtle and less obviously battle-oriented. It is also interesting to note that they pledge to use what is at hand, the natural features of the battlefield, while the Druids have promised to manifest something that is not present and the sorcerers to directly influence the warriors physically. This may hint at the nature of the differences between the types of magic each group uses.

For a modern Irish Polytheist seeking to incorporate magic into Reconstructionism you may decide to focus on one of these three approaches – asarlaí, draíodóir, or Draoi. Or you may prefer to blend the three together, or avoid any such set divisions and focus more on folk magic, ancient and more modern.

The Rosc – Spoken Spells in Irish Magic

In studying the myths and wider Irish folk magic one particular type of magic is commonly found – the rosc. Rosc is defined as a rhetorical composition or chant, although the electronic Dictionary of the Irish Language (eDIL) suggests that the original term in Old Irish may have been rosg, because rosc cannot be traced further back than late medieval documents (eDIL, n.d.). It appears in early manuscripts as rosg catha, referring specifically to battle magic, and later as rosc catha with the same meaning; interestingly rosc also means 'eye' (eDIL, n.d.; O Donaill, 1977). The plural of rosc is roisc, although in modern Druidic vernacular it appears as roscanna; roisc do not generally rhyme, but rely on alliteration instead (eDIL, n.d.). Examples of roscanna are usually seen as battle magics, where the speaker is in a conflict and is using the chant to overcome the enemy in some way. However, there are also examples of roscanna used for other purposes such as blessing or sleep. In mythology Druids are said to be able to create illusions, heal, find the truth of a situation, advise, interpret dreams and curse with the use of roscanna (O hOgain, 1991).

Reciting a rosc may be accompanied by specific actions, such as when we see Lugh reciting a rosc for his army, while circling them with one eye closed, one arm behind his back, and on one leg, a type of ritual pose known as the corrguineacht. The corrguineacht itself is usually associated with cursing, perhaps relating the pose to the Fomorians who are sometimes described as having one leg, arm, and eye, although the name corrguineacht is sometimes translated as Crane Posture. O Tuathail translates it as Crane Prayer (O Tuathail, 1993).

While engaged in this corrguineacht Lugh chants:

Fight a slaughterous battle! There is fierce battle, a contentious, cutting army contending before armies of phantoms, men of the land beware. Aligning to truth without choice, following furies. Bursting forth, overthrowing, dividing, black truth: little white death-ring, Hale! Hale! Woe! Woe! Sinister! Fierceness! A sanctified omen after cloud-shadows our fame will be spread through armies by triple skilled Druids. I am not reduced by battles at borders: wounding, matched, slender-speared, sky ravaging, deadly brilliance, burning, greatly subduing them, greatly thundering, the sun rises. Asking each of them, in the presence of Ogma and also in the presence of sky and earth, in the presence of sun and moon. A band of warriors is my company for you. My army is a great army, ramparts here, fleet-footed, seething, strong-guarding, choosing, may we fight a slaughterous battle! Fight![23]

Rosc are also generally spoken in the present tense, a clear difference from most modern magical chants, which tend to use the future tense. Generally the speaker of the rosc states what they want as if it already is. When a rosc does use the future tense the person speaking is not asking for something to come to pass but stating that it will come to pass. For example when Amergin invokes the bounty of Ireland he says:

Fishful the ocean,
prolific in bounty the land,
an explosion of fish,
fish beneath wave

in currents of water
flashing brightly,
from hundredfolds of salmon
which are the size of whales,
song of a harbor of fames,
an explosion of fish,
fishful the sea.
(O Tuathail, 1993).

This demonstrates not only the use of tense, but also two other qualities of roscanna: the emphasis on descriptive terms and the repetition of the first line, or a variation on it, as the final line. The descriptive nature of roscanna works with the alliterative pattern; along with the repetition of specific lines this reinforces the poetic nature of these chants. Some roscanna, such as Amergin's Invocation of Ireland, also follow a pattern of repeating the end of one line as the beginning of the next line (see example below).

Roscanna also rely on the speaker's own personal power, rather than appeals to higher powers or forces. Someone reciting a rosc is using their own energy and will to enforce their words. We can see this in an excerpt from the rosc Mogh Ruith recites against the King's Druids:

I turn, I re-turn
not but I turn nuclei of darkness
I turn verbal spells, I turn speckled spells,
I turn purities of form,
I turn high, I turn mightily,
I turn each adversity,
I turn a hill to subside....
(O Tuathail, 1993)

O Tuathail suggests that 'turn' in this context means 'transform', which seems logical. We can see the same pattern of invoking personal power in the Song of Amergin, the opening section of which begins each line with the phrase 'I am'. Although a rosc can also be used to invoke the power within an object this is still generally done with an emphasis on the speaker's own personal power calling to what they are invoking. Several examples of this are:

Amergin's Invocation of Ireland
I request the land of Ireland
coursed is the wild sea
wild the crying mountains
crying the generous woods
generous in showers...
(O Tuathail, 1993)

Mogh Ruith's Magic Stone
I request my stone of conflagration.
Be it no ghost of theft.
Be it a blaze that will fight sages
...My fire stone which delves pain
Be it a red serpent which sorrows...
(O Tuathail, 1993)

There are examples of roscanna that rely on invoking a higher power as well, but these appear to be less common. It is possible that the folk magic charms we have today are based on the same principles as the Druidic roscanna, although the modern folk charms more often invoke higher Powers.

In a modern context a rosc can be used for any purpose needed by the speaker. The generally rules of forming a rosc should be followed: alliteration, highly descriptive terms, repetition, and speaking in the present with personal power. If desired or required specific actions can be included as well. An example of this for protection would be:

I am safe, secure, and protected,
Protected from injury and ill-will
From danger and destruction
From all hurt and harm
My magic is an armor, impenetrable,
that turns away all attacks
Turns them to the encompassing earth
Wide and deep, she takes them
transforms them from harm to healing
So that what is sent against me
Becomes a blessing and boon
Protected from injury and ill-will
I am safe, secure, and protected.

Cursing in the Irish Tradition

Although sometimes seen as a controversial topic, there is ample evidence of cursing in Irish folklore and mythology. Cursing might be used as a form of justice, such as we see in the use of satire, or as a punishment and often could only be removed by meeting specific conditions. One method of 'testing' for a curse was to bring a hedgehog near the person and see how it reacted. If its spikes stood up then it was a sure sign of bewitchment (Wilde, 1991).

In mythology we see the use of cursing to force a person to change shape and live as an animal. In the story of Fionn, for example, we see his wife Sabhdh turned into a deer when she is cursed by a spurned suitor; he uses a wand to change her shape. We also see a curse of transformation in the story of the children of Lir, where the children are turned into swans, and in the story of Etain, where Etain is cursed into the form of a butterfly (or moth). Often in these cases the curses can only be lifted under a set of very particular circumstances.

A common type of cursing appearing in literature, and one for which there were later Brehon laws, was satire. Satire is a type of spoken curse that could be laid against a person by a Bard or File in order to affect their life. The most well known example might be the satire against Bres, which cost him the kingship of the Tuatha Dé Danann. Satire could be used against those who had done something – such as Bres – to deserve being punished, but could also be used unfairly against a person and it is that sort that there were later laws against. It was believed that if a poet unfairly spoke a satire then he or she would have a disfiguring blemish – a literal mark of shame – appear on his or her face.

There is archaeological evidence of the use of curse tablets in the Celtic world. Often found at shrine sites the tablets of lead and pewter are engraved with curses describing exactly who and why and usually invoking a specific power (Green, 1997). The existing examples often seek to use the curse to exact justice in a situation, such as retribution for a theft. These curse tablets have been found at the sites of healing shrines, temples, and in springs, and appear written in Latin and Gaulish (Green, 1997).

Some folk curses include the use of sympathetic magic; one such folk method of cursing involves the use of an effigy made of wax, clay, or a similar material, into which thorns or pins can be driven (McNeill, 1956; Evans, 1957). After being made to look like the intended victim the figure would first be pierced with the sharp objects, then would either be placed in a stream where the running water could wear it away or burned in a fire (McNeill, 1956). This type of curse is intended to create a wasting illness or general ill health in the victim (Evans, 1957).

Additionally there are a few other kinds of miscellaneous cursing. In one example Lady Wilde writes of the practice of ritually burying an ear of corn with the intent that as the corn decays the person being cursed will suffer (Wilde, 1991). McNeill mentions the use of a witch-bone, a hollow deer bone with a bog oak ring around it through which blood is poured to ill-wish a person (McNeill, 1956).

It was generally believed that to walk counterclockwise around a person or property could create a curse, particularly when combined with intent or a spoken curse. Finally there is the practice of using stones to curse others. One method is to hold a cursing stone in your left hand and turn it around three times counter clockwise against a person (O hOgain, 1999). Another is to use a spoken curse against someone while building a stone cairn against them, which Carmichael calls a cairn of malediction (Carmichael, 1900).

In Irish culture there are many methods of cursing, and an equal number of protections and counter-curses. Cursing itself was seen as a serious action and a breach of social order, but could also offer power to the powerless. There was a deeply rooted belief that to set a curse without a good cause would bring negative repercussions on the curse caster, which can be seen in the beliefs around satire. In a modern setting using any of these curses should only be done with great caution and after great thought is given to the need and risk.

Verifying Practical UPG

It wouldn't be right to discuss magic and mysticism and not discuss personal numinous experiences, often labeled UPG. Reconstruction tends to have a reputation for rejecting such gnosis, but that is somewhat undeserved. In reality it isn't that we reject UPG, but that we apply the same standards of discernment to it that we do to any source. This leads to the common question in relation to UPG of how to know if the gnosis you get is good or not. A basic rule of thumb is to take the information you get and double check it, whether that's checking it against mythology or other types of fact checking.

I tend to be involved in a lot of mystical activities that result in UPG. Sometimes on purpose, sometimes not so much. The result is the same though, information that comes into my head from outside and then requires some sort of verification. I almost never utilize a UPG without some kind of checking, and when it is checked I find that while some of it turns out to be contradicted (in other words just my head talking to myself) some of it turns out to be even more interesting than I realized at first.

One example is the phrase 'Mache mind', which I had stuck in my head for several days. I knew it was from the *Táin Bó Cúailnge* and thought that it meant 'halidom of Macha'; I had a visionary experience where I saw a sword with those words engraved on it. I initially thought the message of the vision was that the sword was a sacred object of Macha, which is one layer of meaning and is true, but after several days of this stuck in my head I finally double checked the word mind. It turns out mind in Old Irish also means 'blade, weapon', so that Mache mind also means Macha's blade. As soon as I learned that it felt as if something clicked and the phrase stopped being stuck in my head. Part of the UPG had to do with me understanding the vision and the phrase on the sword, and that meant getting out of my own assumption.

I recently also had a UPG experience involving herbal knowledge. Herbs are not my forte.[24] I was looking for an oil to use in a cleansing bath and was feeling like I needed something particular. I tried to open myself up using an Irish seership method[25] to find out which one I needed. On the store display my eyes went to rosemary oil, but I dismissed it. I knew that rosemary was burned to cleanse sick rooms after illnesses, but not much else about it and that wasn't the sort of thing I was looking for. Nonetheless I kept feeling that rosemary was what I needed and when I tried picking out a different bottle the next one I grabbed from a different area of the display was also rosemary, even though there shouldn't have been two bottles (according to the store owner). I gave in and went to look up the uses of rosemary to see if this little UPG had anything to it, and it turned out that yes indeed rosemary is used in cleansing and purification according to two different books on magical uses of herbs.

Both of these are just small things, but I hope they demonstrate the way that different types of UPG can be researched and double checked. Instead of just trusting the random information we get in visions, dreams, and intuition we can take the time to see what deeper meanings might be behind them. Sometimes they may come to nothing. Other times they may prove out, and then you will know going forward how much depth your gnosis had.

Chapter 6

Hot Topics: Race, Cultural Appropriation, and Sexuality

Secht asa midithar duine: cruth ocus cenél, tír ocus trebad, dán ocus indmas ocus indracus.
On the Manners and Customs of the Ancient Irish
(Seven things on which a person is estimated: form and family, land and house, skill and possessions and integrity.)

Racism and Cultural Appropriation

Paganism in many ways reflects the contemporary trends of culture: in the 1960s and 70s it was feminism and women's empowerment, in the 1980s and 90s it was individual empowerment. In the past ten years, and more so now, I've seen an increase in the focus on the ideas of ethnicity, race, and cultural appropriation within paganism.

Issues of culture and race are complex and this is no less true in paganism than it is in the wider culture. On the one hand people often seek, through spirituality, to reconnect to their own history and roots, to gain a sense of belonging, and this can sometimes lead to a focus on culture through ancestry. Certainly this is the case with most Reconstructionist faiths, which often emphasize both specific culture and ancestral connections and veneration. Feeling connected to ancestry through religion teaches us to be proud – proud of our ancestors' trials, struggles, and successes. Generally this is a good thing; we should be proud of our ancestry and our cultural history. This can become a problem though when that pride and the desire to feel that sense of belonging becomes a sense of possession, as if that religion belongs exclusively to any one group or people. In Irish paganism I see this when people are dismissed as not really Irish pagans, as if their opinions have no or less value if they don't live in Ireland, speak a Celtic language, or have recent Irish ancestry. In some cases it can be less subtly expressed in outright racism[26] and exclusion of non-Europeans from groups. I've heard of it in other faiths as well, from Wicca to Hellenismios, when one person tells another that they have no right to that religion because it belongs to another culture. It is all rooted in the idea that these beliefs are ours and we must protect them by keeping out the unworthy or those who might threaten the quality of what is ours. It's not always expressed that way, but that's the core idea behind it; we have something special that belongs to us and we must keep it safe from anyone who isn't us.

The big, obvious problem with this is: who gets to decide who owns the culture? Who can say what amount of heritage is enough? Oh people try, certainly, but it all comes down to personal opinion and assumption, no matter how prettily they attempt to dress it up as the will of the Gods. How far back does someone's ancestry have to go for it to be enough? Can skin color really be a measure of heritage when it tells you nothing practical about that person's ethnicity? My heritage, like many Americans, is complex, so what cultures am I entitled to? What cultures am I excluded from?

Belonging to a culture, sharing its beliefs, was always based on far more than skin color and birth. History tells us that the Vikings intermarried with the Irish; that our ancestors, as they moved into new lands, intermarried with the people already there. The Gods were your Gods because they were the ones you honored, the ones you prayed to and offered to, not because you passed some litmus test of color or ancestry. The culture was your culture because it was what you lived, valued, and passed on. This was true in the past so in a modern multicultural, multi-ethnic society what place could racism possible have?

Or, to summarize, racism is stupid and has no place anywhere in anything.

On the other hand we have cultural appropriation, a very popular term right now that is often horribly misunderstood and misused. Taken from sociology, cultural appropriation – also called cultural borrowing – is a natural and normal cultural process wherein one culture adopts beliefs, practices, or items from another culture usually with modifications. The western idea of karma is a cultural appropriation from the east, for example. Cultural appropriation, in and of itself, is not inherently a bad thing. However, it can be so when the culture being taken from is a minority culture and the one doing the taking is a dominant one. In such a case appropriation can often lead to the loss of the original culture's belief or practice as it is subsumed and eventually discarded in favor of the dominant culture's version. The fear of that happening is often cited in cultural forms of paganism, including Irish and Norse, as grounds to speak out against or reject concepts taken from a specific culture and redefined by more popular modern pagan traditions. For example, a reiki practitioner took the Irish Ogham and created what they call Celtic reiki, something that is seen as appropriation by some Irish pagans and some traditional reiki practitioners. The taking of the four Celtic fire festivals for use in the neopagan wheel of the year is sometimes viewed as appropriation in the same way. James Arthur Ray's appropriation and misuse of sweat lodges is another, more tragic, example. Cultural appropriation is a very complex subject, though, because it is a natural cultural process and can occur organically – the use of sage smudge, for example – so that not all appropriation is necessarily bad.

In academia, cultural appropriation may be divided into different categories, which can include exchange, dominance, exploitation, and transculturation (Rogers, 2006). Exchange and transculturation are positive while dominance and exploitation are negative. Culture itself is built on a process of interaction with and reciprocal appropriation of other cultures, which over times creates cultural exchange (Rogers, 2006). Generally when cultural appropriation is discussed in paganism, what is actually meant is cultural exploitation, the taking of aspects of a minority culture by a dominant one for the advantage of the dominant culture. This is a touchy issue, but as modern pagans we cannot simply say that we will not ever use or include anything that isn't originally from our culture or that no one else has a right to what we consider ours, particularly since, as I already discussed, it can be very difficult to decide who has a right to what; certainly the ancient pagans freely incorporated material from others in what would be seen as cultural exchange. On the other hand we should be respectful of other cultures and do everything we can to avoid what amounts to cultural plagiarism. My personal rule of thumb is to look at the context of the original and then how it is being applied outside that context; if it seems to be respectfully done then I am okay with it, if it seems to be done superficially, without respect, or understanding then I am not okay with it. We can use Samhain as an example: in modern paganism some people have begun to incorporate genuinely Irish pagan practices including a food offering to the fairies. I would not have an issue with this when the person researchers it and understands why it was done and historically how, even if their version is different from mine – candy instead of caudle, perhaps – but if the person simply hears that it was a practice to offer to the fairies, doesn't bother to learn anything about it, and offers something that would traditionally be offensive – spoiled food or leftovers, perhaps – then I would see that as inappropriate. When you come across genuine appropriation the best way to fight it may be to educate people about the real beliefs and practices and the history, the roots, from which they have come.

We are all, ultimately, seeking the same thing. As human beings we all want to be happy; as religious practitioners we all want to find spiritual fulfillment. The differences between us are, literally, only skin deep, and yet culture can shape us in profound ways that go far beyond outward differences and do deserve to be honored. Be proud of who you are and where you've come from and respect the journey that's brought you this far, but always respect those who are walking along with you as well by honoring the things we have in common as well as our differences.

Ní neart go cur le chéile.[27]

Sexuality in Ancient Ireland

This falls into the category of frequently asked questions, because I regularly see people wondering what the ancient Irish or Celtic view of homosexuality was. The short answer seems to be that prior to Christianity it was not remarkable. Let's take a look at the long answer: There is very little direct mention of homosexuality in the ancient Irish mythology or stories (Power, 1976).

Some people might decide this is indicative of a lack of homosexuality in general, but it appears that in fact the opposite was the case, that it may have been seen as accepted and unremarkable. Partially we can draw this conclusion because we know that societies that did strongly prohibit same-sex pairings for any reason tended to be very vocal about that fact and we find references to being the submissive sexual partner frequently used as an insult against men in such cultures, such as the Norse. However, that is lacking in the Irish[28] and the Celts more generally, indicating that same-sex relations were not viewed as shameful or, one may assume, abnormal. We can also draw this conclusion using evidence from secondary sources, in this case Greek observers.

One indicator of the acceptance of homosexuality in Celtic culture is a comment by Aristotle in his *Politics* where he mentions the way that the Gauls openly approved of sexual relationships between men (Freeman, 2002). Similarly Diodorus also describes the open way that Gaulish men had sexual relations with each other, in a way that seemed to baffle the

Greeks because the Gauls favored relationships between equals and were not concerned with beauty or age (Freeman, 2002). This is noteworthy because this Mediterranean culture itself engaged in forms of homosexual practice so they would not have included mention of it among the Celts as propaganda implying moral judgment; rather it was mentioned because the classical historians found the Celts lack of discernment concerning partners[29] and lack of concern about social order – reflected in taking partners among equals instead of younger men – to reflect barbarism. Although this evidence relates to the Gaulish Celts and not the Irish Celts it is indicative of the wider cultural views that seemed to be held within Celtic societies.

We do have some indication within Irish mythology that same-sex pairings were accepted and not seen as unusual and this comes from the *Táin Bó Cúailnge* and the relationship of Ferdiad and Cu Chulain. During the fighting Cu Chulain has set himself up to block the attacking army and is taking on challengers one by one. Queen Medb convinces his foster brother Ferdiad to fight against him, much to Cu Chulain's dismay. When the two first meet on the battle field Cu Chulain says to Ferdiad: 'We were heart-companions once; We were comrades in the woods; We were men that shared a bed.' Ferdiad responds that that time was long ago and insists on fighting (Windsch, 1905). We can further see the closeness of their relationship by looking at the mourning poem of Cu Chulain after he kills Ferdiad. He laments Ferdiad's death with these words: 'I loved the noble way you blushed, and loved your fine, perfect form. I loved your blue clear eye, your way of speech, your skillfulness.' (Kinsella, 1969). He goes on to praise Ferdiad's beauty further as well as his weapon skill and lament that Ferdiad was led to his death by the promise of marriage to Medb's daughter. Many people see in this passage the lament of one lover for another, something that is consistent with the practices discussed by Aristotle and Diodorus of Celtic warriors taking each other as lovers, and with Cu Chulain's own comment that they were 'heart-companions' and 'men who shared a bed'.

There is also mention of homosexuality in the Brehon Laws. One reason that a woman may lawfully divorce her husband is if he refuses her bed in favor of a male lover (Kelly, 2005). Although this is often taken as prohibitions against homosexuality, it is important to understand the passage in context and to realize that it is not homosexuality as a practice that is being spoken against, but the denial of a potential child to the wife. It specifies that it is only acceptable grounds for divorce if the husband denies his wife's bed in favor of his male lover's, and this is listed along with infertility, and being too fat for intercourse, making it clear that it is not the sexual preference per se but the lack of fulfilling marriage terms – i.e. providing a child. Additionally it is worth considering that there is a story in the book of Leinster which references two woman who are lovers; one woman becomes pregnant after lying with the other who had just had sex with a male partner (Bitel, 1996). What is most important about this story is that neither woman was punished or shamed in any way for their actions, indicating that women taking female lovers was not seen in a negative way (Bitel, 1996).

In conclusion what evidence we do have seems to make it clear that sexual preference was not noteworthy until Christian mores took over. Warriors in Celtic Gaul were noted by the Greeks to take male lovers and there are at least echoes of this practice in the relationship between Cu Chulain and Ferdiad. The law texts also address this in a way that does not condemn the act itself, but only the nullification of a contract as a result of denying a female partner. Looking at the evidence in its entirety, scanty as it may be, I think it's safe to conclude that bisexuality was not considered remarkable, nor were homosexual relationships. Marriage was a complex contractual affair regulated by law and intended to produce heirs, but love and sexual relations did not seem to necessarily always share this focus, nor an emphasis on heterosexuality.

Modern Irish Polytheism, in my experience, is accepting of all types of sexuality involving consenting adults.

Chapter 7

Conclusion

Tosach eólais imchomarc Bríathra Flainn Fína maic Ossu
(The beginning of knowledge is inquiry)

Irish Reconstruction Polytheism is about learning as much as we can about what the ancient culture was like and what the religion was like in order to bring the core of it forward in a workable modern way. We are not trying to bring ourselves back or create a backwards looking religion, rather we want to envision what that ancient paganism would have grown into had it not been interrupted. By researching and using archaeology, anthropology, history, mythology, and linguistics we can gain a better understanding of the beliefs and practices that existed thousands of years ago and find the best ways to bring that forward in a viable modern way.

Irish Polytheism is not a static faith; it is not only about picking out bits and pieces of old pagan practices to use. Achieving a thorough grounding in the ancient culture and the principles of modern reconstruction allows people to then create new material in the spirit of the old material; songs, poems, invocations, rituals, and all the other essentials. No religion can survive long if it is not living and growing and that is equally true of Reconstructionism. Now it is true that new material has to be in line with the old, because part of reconstruction is not introducing foreign elements, but the world we live in today is very different from the world thousands of years ago – if we can't create a religion that is modern and that is adapted for the modern world, then really, what's the point?

Our approach is a viable modern faith that is rooted in an ancient pagan faith, brought forward as we envision it if it had never stopped being practiced. Each individual and every group will have their own ideas on what that would look like depending on their own views and interpretations of the available material, creating a very similar situation to what it was like back then when each tribe had its own particular ways within the larger culture. Nonetheless we all share a common goal and a common vision that should hold us together as a community. We keep the core cultural values, the main religious practices and beliefs, and we use critical thinking and inspiration, along with a deep understanding of the historical culture, to adapt the surviving material and to create new material in the spirit of the old. Because reconstruction is not just about the book-knowledge or the research – it's about actively living the spirituality we find there.

Appendix A

Pronunciation Guide

Emphasis will be on the first syllable in both modern and old Irish.

Modern Irish

Aos si – ace shee
Áine – AWN-yuh
Airmeith – AIR-uh-meh
Badhbh – Bive or bayv
Bealtaine – BYALL-tin-eh
Brighid – Breedj
Daghdha – DAY-duh
Daoine si – DEE-neh shee
Dian Cécht – Deen Cayht
Fliodhais – FLOH-deesh
Imbolg – IHM-bulg
Lugh – Loo
Lúnasa – LOO-nuh-suh
Macha – MAH-kuh
Manannán – MAH-nah-nawn
Miach – MEE-uhk
Mórríoghan – MORE-ree-uhn
Nuada – NOO-ah-duh
Óengus – AYN-gehs
Oghma – OH-mah
Samhain – SOW-en
Si – shee
Tuatha Dé Danann – TOO-ah-hah djay DAH-nahn

Old Irish

Áine – AHN-yeh
Airmed – AIR-uh-veth
Badb – BAH-thv
Beltine – BELL-tihn-eh
Brig – Brihg
Dagda – DAHG-thuh
Dien Cécht – DEE-uhn Cay(k)t
Flidais – FLIH-dahsh
Lug – Luhg
Lugnasad – LUHG-nahs-ahd
Macha - MOCK-uh
Manannán – MAH-nahn-awn
Miach – MIH-uhk
Morrigan – MOR-reeg-ahn
Nuada – NOO-ah-thah
Ogma – OHG-mah
Oimelc – OH-melk
Samain – SAH-man

Modern Names for Irish Polytheism

Ildiachas Gaelach – ILL-dee-uh-huhs GAY-luhk Gaelic Polytheism
Ildiachas na hÉireann – ILL-dee-uh-huhs nuh h-AY-rehn Polytheism of Ireland
Céile na nDéithe – KAY-leh nuh NAY-ih-heh Servant of the Gods
Págánacht – PAW-gaw-nuhkt Pagan

Appendix B

Recommended Reading for Irish Polytheists

The Apple Branch: A Path to Celtic Ritual by Alexei Kondratiev – not Irish specific, but a must-read for the history of the various holidays; also full of important mythology and folklore.

The Lore of Ireland: An Encyclopedia of Myth, Legend and Romance by Dáithí O hOgain – essential quick reference for different Irish material, especially deities, heroes, places, and holidays.

The Sacred Isle by Dáithí O hOgain – discusses Irish religion from pre-Christian times through conversion.

A Practical Guide to Irish Spirituality by Lora O'Brien – a little bit of everything about Irish pagan spirituality written in a very engaging way.

Druidry and the Ancestors by Nimue Brown – not specifically Irish, but an excellent look at how to incorporate ancestor honoring into modern practice.

The CR FAQs – the best basic start to understanding what reconstruction is from a Celtic viewpoint.

The Lebor Gabála Érenn – the story of the invasions of Ireland by the Gods and spirits and eventually humans. The Tuatha da Danann are usually seen as the Gods of ancient Ireland so this book is important in understanding them.

Cath Maige Tuired – the story of the battle of the Tuatha Dé Danann with the Fomorians.

The Year in Ireland by K. Danaher – an overview of holidays and folk practices throughout the year.

The Silver Bough (all four volumes) by F. MacNeil – Scottish, but extremely useful for understanding folk practices and beliefs.

Fairy and Folktales of the Irish Peasantry by Yeats – a look at folklore and belief relating to the Fair Folk.

Lady with a Mead Cup by Enright – useful look at ritual structure and society in Celtic culture.

Celtic Flame: an Insider's Guide to Irish Pagan Tradition by Aedh Rua – one perspective on reconstructing the beliefs and practices of the pagan Irish in a modern setting. Although this approach will not be to everyone's taste it is a valuable example of how it can be done.

A Child's Eye View of Irish Paganism by Blackbird O'Connell – written for children aged eight to 12, this book is an effective, short introduction to the basic beliefs, Gods, and practices of Irish paganism.

Where the Hawthorn Grows – my own book, but one that touches on some important basics of practicing Irish Reconstructionism.

Celtic Gods and Heroes by Sjoestedt – discusses both the Gods and tidbits of folklore and mythology.

Celtic Seers Sourcebook by J. Matthews – a good resource for reconstructing Irish and more generally Celtic seership and mystic practices. This book includes some seminal essays including Chadwick's 'Imbas Forosnai' and Best's 'Prognostication from the Raven and the Wren'.

A Circle of Stones by E. R. Laurie – an excellent book on meditation and prayer practices in Celtic Reconstruction with an Irish focus.

Teagasca: The Instructions of Cormac Mac Airt by C. Lee Vermeers – a new translation of an old Irish wisdom text that provides essential insight into living honorably.

Air n-Aithesc – a biannual peer reviewed CR journal that often includes Irish Polytheism-themed articles of interest to modern Irish Polytheist Reconstructionists. It can be found at http://ciannai2.wix.com/air-n-aithesc

Appendix C

Myth titles in Both Languages

Within the text I have used the names of the stories and myths in Irish or Old Irish. There are, however, translations of them available, usually under an Anglicized name so I will provide a list of both:

Aislinge Óenguso – The Dream of Oengus
Banshenchus – The Lore of Women
Cath Maige Tuired Cunga – First Battle of Moytura
Cath Maige Tuired – Battle of Moytura
Cóir Anmann – Fitness of Names
De Gabáil in t-Sída – The Taking of the Sidhe
Genemain Áeda Sláne – The Birth of Aedh Slaine
Lebor Gabála Érenn – The Book of Invasions
Táin Bó Cúailnge – The Cattle Raid of Cooley
Táin Bó Regamna – The Cattle Raid of Regamna
Tochmarc Emire – The Wooing of Emer
Tochmarc Étaine – The Wooing of Etain

Bibliography

The Battle of Mag Mucrama http://www.maryjones.us/ctexts /mucrama.html

The Battle of Crimna http://www.maryjones.us/ctexts /cathcrinna.html

Banshenchus (nd) Retrieved from http://www.maryjones.us/ctexts /banshenchus.html

Best, R., (2007) *The Settling of the Manor of Tara* http://www. ucd.ie/tlh/text/rib.eriu.4.001.text.html

Bitel, L., (1996) *Land of Women*

Briggs, Katharine (1978) *The Vanishing People: Fairy Lore and Legends*

Clancy., S., Jewell, K., Kondratiev, A., Nicholson, F., and Wood, H., (2005) *By Land, Sea, and Sky*. Retrieved from http:// homepage.eircom.net/~shae/contents.htm

Daimler, M., (2014). *Pagan Portals: The Morrigan*

Danaher (1972) *The Year in Ireland*

eDIL (n.d.) Electronic Dictionary of the Irish Language. Retrieved from http://edil.qub.ac.uk/dictionary/search.php

Ellis, P., (1987) *Dictionary of Irish Mythology*

Evans, E., (1957) *Irish Folk Ways*

Freeman, P., (2002) *War, Women, and Druids*

Gray, E., (1983) *Cath Maige Tuired*

Green, M (1992) *Dictionary of Celtic Myth and Legends*

Gulermovich Epstein, A., (1998) *War Goddess: The Morrígan and her Germano-Celtic Counterparts*. Electronic version,#148, September, 1998. Retrieved from http://web.archive. org/web/20010616084231/members.loop.com/~musofire/diss/

Gundarsson, K., (2007) *Elves, Wights, and Trolls*

Gwynn, E., (1906) *Metrical Dindshenchas*

Hall, A., (2005) *Getting Shot of Elves: Healing, Witchcraft, and Fairies in the Scottish Witchcraft Trials*

Hopman, E., (2008) *A Druid's Herbal of Sacred Tree Medicine*. Rochester: Destiny Books

Keating, G., (1857) *Foras Feasa ar Éirinn*

Kelly, F., (2005) *A Guide to Early Irish Law*

Kinsella, T., (1969) The Tain

Koch, J., (2003) *The Celtic Heroic Age*

Kondratiev, A. (1998) *Apple Branch: A Path to Celtic Ritual*

Jones, M., (n.d.) *The Birth of Aedh Slaine*. Retrieved from http://www.maryjones.us/ctexts/aedhslaine.html

Jones, M., (n.d.) *Ogma*. Retrieved from http://www.maryjones.us/jce/ogma.html

Laurie, E., (1996) *The Cauldron of Poesy*

Leabhar na h-Uidre (nd) Retrieved from http://www.maryjones.us/ctexts/flidais.html

Leahy, A., (1906) *Heroic Romances of Ireland*

Macalister, R., (1940) *Lebor Gabála Érenn*, volumes 3 and 4

MacDonald, L., (1993) People of the Mounds. Dalriada Magazine http://deoxy.org/h_mounds.htm

MacKillop, J., (1998) *A Dictionary of Celtic Mythology*

MacNeill, M., (1962) *The Festival of Lúnasa*

McCormick, F., (2010) *Ritual Feasting in Iron Age Ireland*

McNeill, F., (1956) *The Silver Bough*, volume 1

McNeill, F., (1959) *The Silver Bough*, volume 2

Matthews, J., (1999) *Celtic Seer's Sourcebook*

Matthews, J., (1997) *The Druid's Sourcebook*

Meyers, K., (1906) *The Triads of Ireland*

Meyer, K., (1910) *The Wooing of Emer*

Monaghan, P., (2004) *Encyclopedia of Celtic Mythology and Folklore*

Monro, D., (1695) *A Description of the Western Isles of Scotland*

Nodens (2012). Websters Online Dictionary. http://www.websters-online-dictionary.org/definitions /Nodens

O Donaill, N., (1977) *Focloir Gaeilge-Bearla*

O'Dubhain, S., (1997) *The Elements of the Dúile*

O'Dubhain, S., (2003) *Celts, Karma and Reincarnation*

O Grady, H,. (1892) *Silva Gadelica*

O hOgain, D., (1991) *Myth, Legend, and Romance*

O hOgain, D., (1999) *The Sacred Isle*

O hOgain, D., (2006) *The Lore of Ireland*

O hOgain, D., (1995) *Irish Superstitions*

O Suilleabhain, S., (1967) *Nosanna agus Piseoga na nGael*

O Tuathail, S., (1993) *The Excellence of Ancient word: Druid Rhetoric from Ancient Irish Tales*

Power, P., (1976) *Sex and Marriage in Ancient Ireland*

Rogers, R., (2006) From Cultural Exchange to Transculturation: A Review and Reconceptualization of Cultural Appropriation. Communication Theory, vol 16, issue 4

Rolleston, T., (1911). *Myths and Legends of the Celtic Race*

Sanas Cormac (n.d.) http://www.asnc.cam.ac.uk/irishglossaries/texts.php?versionID=9&ref=150#150

Sjoedsedt, M., (2000) *Celtic Gods and Heroes*

Stokes, W., (1926) *The Second Battle of Moytura*

The Ballad of Tam Lin http://www.sacred-texts.com/neu/eng/
• child/ch039.htm

The Sí, the Tuatha de Danaan, and the Fairies in Yeats's Early Works http://www.csun.edu/~hceng029/yeats/funaro.html

Tochmarc Emire (n.d.) http://www.ucc.ie/celt/published/G301021/

Wentz, W. Y. (1966) *The Fairy-Faith in Celtic Countries*

Wilde, F., (1991) *Irish Cures, Mystic Charms and Superstitions*

Windisch, E., (1905) *Tain Bo Cualgne*

The Wooing of Emer

Yeats, W. B. (nd) *Celtic Twilight*

Endnotes

1 Ceisiwr Serith has an interesting book called *Back to the Beginnings: Re-inventing Wicca* which is, to all intents and purposes, an attempt to reconstruct Indo-European religious witchcraft.

2 Unless otherwise noted all translations are the author's.

3 Commonly known, somewhat inaccurately, as the Sapir-Whorf hypothesis.

4 Please note that the older myths are written in Sengoidelc, or Old Irish, which is an older version of the language than modern Irish. It is certainly an option to learn both of them if you'd like, however you should be aware that Sengoidelc is more useful for reading the older mythology while modern Irish is better for connecting to the modern culture. If your main focus is connecting to the modern Irish culture then the modern language is the better choice; if your goal is to read the mythology for yourself and not rely on translations you will need the Old Irish.

5 Unverified personal gnosis (UPG), or as Lora O'Brien puts it (and I like better) unique personal gnosis. I've also been known to refer to this as personal numinous experience, but PNE isn't as catchy of an acronym. In Irish and Celtic Reconstruction this is also sometimes referred to as aislíng.

6 Clui may be an ancient name for the area of Limerick that Áine presides over (O hOgain, 2006).

7 Crom Cruach is a primordial deity also known as Crom Dubh who appears in Irish mythology as an antagonistic figure; his role at Lunasa is that of the chaotic force trying to steal the harvest or keep it from people (MacNeill, 1962).

8 Blood offerings are controversial and many people are strongly against the entire concept. There is no requirement to do them. However, some do find them appropriate to offer

for the battle Goddesses. In this context the blood offered should be your own, either using sterile lancets or spilled during martial activities.

9 Caoine is anglicized as keen or keening and is a formalized ritual weeping and crying.

10 This story is somewhat controversial as Dian Cécht heals Nuadha by giving him a silver arm only to have his son Miach, seven years later, heal the original arm allowing Nuadha to become king again. Dian Cécht challenges Miach and kills him. Many people see this story as a tale of jealousy; however, I believe that Miach was disrupting the right order, fírinne, of things by healing Nuada when it was Lugh who was meant to be king next and lead the rebellion against the Fomorians.

11 Kine is an archaic word for cows.

12 The folk beliefs vary across Ireland in ways that can be contradictory, so that the tree that should never be cut and brought inside in one area, lest it draw the Fair Folk, is the same one recommended elsewhere to protect against them. Similarly one area might believe that keeping dirty water in the home draws fairies and grants them entrance while another area believes this water drives them away. This can make it difficult to say almost anything with absolute certainty as there are nearly always exceptions.

13 I recommend reading the article 'Liberalia, Hero-feast of Cu Chulainn' for more on this modern practice https://aediculaantinoi.wordpress.com/2011/03/17/liberalia-hero-feast-of-cu-chulainn/

14 Except the daoine sidhe, as I have a superstition about never saying 'thank you' to them I ask instead that there always be friendship and peace between us.

15 Invoke, despite modern pagan misconceptions of the word, means:

1. To call on (a higher power) for assistance, support, or

inspiration

2. To appeal to or cite in support or justification.

3. To call for earnestly; solicit (http://www.thefreedic tionary.com/invoke)

    I use words based on definition not popular perception or urban-legend style meanings.

16 Old Irish found here http://www.daltai.com/cgi-sys/cgi wrap/daltai/discus/show.pl?tpc=12465&post=10574#POST10 574

17 There may well be variations of this.

18 The term 'kalends' or 'calends' – these words were used to denote the first day of the month for the Roman calendar.

19 Different crops have various tolerances to frost, and this is somewhat dependent on the severity and length of the frost as well. However, it seems safe to say that our ancestors would be highly motivated to get all the crops in by the time they started seeing frost and would consider frost a sign of the end of the harvest season and beginning of winter.

20 For further information on Imbolc traditions and ideas for modern practices see Air n-Aithesc vol 1 iss 1 http://cian nai2.wix.com/air-n-aithesc#!mags/cnec.

21 A literal translation is: 'Belltaine that is lucky fire that is fire of prosperity that is a festival held with two fires Druids made with incantations...making the offspring of the herds receive blessing every year against illness (left hand marginalia – they needed the herds between)'

22 The section on Lunasa is an edited version of an article which previously appeared in my book *Where the Hawthorn Grows*. More in-depth articles on each of the four fire festivals can be found in that book.

23 From Grey's Irish Texts Edition of the *Cath Maige Tuired*: Conid and rocan Lug an cétal-so síos, for lethcois ocus letsúil timchel fer n-Erenn. 'Arotroi* cat comartan! Isin cathirgal robris comlondo forslech-slúaig silsiter ria sluagaib siobrai

iath fer fomnai. Cuifecithai fir gen rogam lentor gala. Fordomaisit, fordomcloisid, forandechraiged, firduib: becc find nomtam (nointam), Fó! Fó! Fé! Fé! Clé! Amainsi! Neofitman-n ier nelscoth- trie trencerdaib druag. Nimcredbod catha fri cricha; nesit- mede midege fornemairces forlúachoir loisces martaltsuides martorainn trogais. Incomairsid fri cech naie, go comair Ogma sachu go comair nem ocus talom, go comair grioan ocus esqu. Dremniadh mo drem-sie duib. Mo sluag so sluag mor murnech mochtsailech bruithe nertirech rogenoir et- dacri ataforroi cath comortai. Aotrai.'

24 Any personal gnosis relating to herbs need to be checked with special care and no herb should ever be used without its safety being ascertained first.

25 I discuss my reconstruction of Irish seership methods in detail in *Pagan Portals: The Morrigan.*

26 Racism is the belief that different races have different abilities and characteristics and race can also be used to describe ethnic groups, including the Irish, English, etc., While we might most often think of racism as the division of people by skin color, it applies equally to the division of people by ethnicity. The infamous 'No Irish Need Apply' signs of 19th century America are examples of that type of racism.

27 'There is no strength without unity.'

28 Rather in the Irish we see insults aimed at people's ancestry, youth/inexperience, courage, and skill at arms.

29 As Diodorus puts it: 'The oddest part about the whole business is that young men don't care at all about appearance and will gladly give their bodies to anyone.' (Freeman, 2002).

MOON
BOOKS

Moon Books invites you to begin or deepen your encounter with Paganism, in all its rich, creative, flourishing forms.